What people  From

Fencing is an amazing sport conveying real values. History is the cradle of our sport. Through tales and movies children have at least once identified with one of their heroes. We must develop this historical link, maintain it and not forget it. Learning history through fencing is very motivational for a child. Learning to learn, our sport is so rich in subtle details and intelligence: self-discipline in respecting the rules, codes often written in the past century; self-confidence in daring to face a comrade; humility in accepting a defeat, accepting a friend's superiority; strength in using this defeat to build future victories.

The real competition only starts after understanding all these values. Then children will be ready for the battle and accept the challenge. In short, this is when they will be ready to face Life. Fencing is an art before being a sport, and the teaching of children should follow this path: to teach and not to train. *From Last to First* will help children to start on this path and help their parents to understand it clearly.

Christian Bauer, Head Coach, Russia; multiple Olympic gold medal-winning coach

Jon Salfield and Daniela Norris's book *From Last to First* provides comprehensive answers to both parents and young fencers regarding their journey in our sport from the beginning. The book reads easily and is full of detailed knowledge which should help in raising the standard and speeding up the development of young fencers. The right kind of parental support is crucial in the participation and success of young people in every sport, and this book captures the very specific requirements for fencing, many of them unique. Such a publication is long overdue and

i

I would recommend this excellent work to every parent and young fencer entering this romantic sport.

Ziemek Wojciechowski, GB Olympic foil coach, winning multiple World Cup and Grand Prix gold medals, and medals at the Senior European and World Championships

As a young fencer who was (and still is!) incredibly passionate about his sport, this comprehensive and intelligent breakdown of how to get the best start in training and competition would have helped me and my family to jump many hurdles and avoid many pitfalls! Full of useful information and insights built up over years of top-level coaching, this is a very valuable resource for any young fencer and their parents.

James Honeybone, 2012 Olympian and British sabre champion

Fencing has become a way of life for our family, and our daughters have benefited so much from the experience. They have become excellent at managing their time, have developed an outstanding work ethic, and have confidence in themselves and their work. They have made friends all over the world through fencing, and the sport has helped both our daughters to attend world-class universities while continuing to fence for their university and country. There is no doubt that this amazing sport, and the conscientious and structured way in which they were introduced to it and have been coached, has had a huge positive impact on our daughters' lives, and will continue to do so for many years to come. This book documents much of the process we and many other families have been through, and clarifies some of the mysteries fencing parents face!

Richard Chart and Margie Mascolino, parents of Yvonne Chart (foil) and Maria Chart (sabre)

Combining the personal experiences of a 'fencing parent' with insights from top GB coach Jon Salfield, alongside experts in sports science and easy-to-understand summaries of relevant research, *From Last to First* is a must-read for every parent whose child has started to fence. It answers many of the questions that a parent new to the sport might have. Whether or not your child does make it all the way from 'Last to First', this book will help you to ensure the experience your child has in fencing is the best it can possibly be.

Georgina Usher, CEO, British Fencing and Grand Prix Épée finalist

For the young fencer it is very important to start in the right way, with good technique, good footwork and the right mentality. This book explains very clearly the right way to think about fencing and training, and is full of the experience of sabre coach Jon Salfield, who is well-known and respected on the international circuit. *From Last to First* is very important reading for any young fencer and their parent in any weapon.

Peter Frohlich, Olympic and World championship medal-winning coach, Hungary

From Last to First

A Parent's Guide to Fencing Success

From Last to First

A Parent's Guide to Fencing Success

Jon Salfield & Daniela I. Norris

CHANGEMAKERS
BOOKS

Winchester, UK
Washington, USA

JOHN HUNT PUBLISHING

First published by Changemakers Books, 2020
Changemakers Books is an imprint of John Hunt Publishing Ltd., No. 3 East Street,
Alresford, Hampshire SO24 9EE, UK
office@jhpbooks.com
www.johnhuntpublishing.com
www.changemakers-books.com

For distributor details and how to order please visit the 'Ordering' section on our website.

Text copyright: Jon Salfield and Daniela I. Norris 2019

ISBN: 978 1 78904 133 0
978 1 78904 134 7 (ebook)
Library of Congress Control Number: 2019933921

A CIP catalogue record for this book is available from the British Library.

Design: Stuart Davies

UK: Printed and bound by CPI Group (UK) Ltd, Croydon, CR0 4YY
US: Printed and bound by Thomson-Shore, 7300 West Joy Road, Dexter, MI 48130

We operate a distinctive and ethical publishing philosophy in
all areas of our business, from our global network of authors to
production and worldwide distribution.

Contents

Foreword

by Richard Cohen

In Molière's play *Le Bourgeois Gentilhomme*, first staged before Louis XIV in 1670, a fencing master pronounces the now-famous dictum, "The whole art of fencing consists in just two things: to hit and not to be hit." That seems sensible enough, but while it applies to épée, it is not true of the modern sabre or foil. Their different rules mean that, if you attack correctly, even if your opponent hits you at the same time, the referee will give you the hit. This means you must be crafty; out-thinking and deceiving your opponent is at the heart of the sport, one of the reasons that fencing is sometimes called 'athletic chess'.

This book is for the new fencer or fencing parent, and is about the sport as a whole, but one of its authors, Jon Salfield, was a sabre fencer (as was I), and his ability to think on his feet marked him out as a top competitor and helps him as a coach and author too. I remember some years ago, well into the autumn of my fencing career, I came up against Jon, then a member of the British team, in the National Championships. Despite his illustrious standing, I noticed he had fallen into certain patterns, movements that he repeated during a bout, and I managed to beat him 5-3. A couple of years later, we met again in the championships, and I was comprehensively beaten 5-0. Jon had simply out-thought me, and if it's not too much of a stretch I would say this thoughtfulness characterises his approach not only to the sport but also the way he coaches. He has reflected deeply about how to teach the art of fencing, and his approach is apparent in this book.

While I was still in my teens, my father (a fine heavyweight boxer in his time) retired from his job early and bought a pub in Cornwall, The White House Inn, just outside Truro, the home town of Jon's fencing club. My father became the county's first chairman of fencing, but there were so few fencers then that meetings were easily accommodated in one of the pub's back rooms. Truro may have been Cornwall's county town, but it still had fewer than 12,000 inhabitants, and fencing was an almost unpractised sport. During his time coaching there, Jon has accomplished a revolution, making Truro a centre of sabre fencing in Britain, with more than 100 members, adept at foil and épée as well as his own weapon of sabre, and with a roster of champions that includes boys and girls, men and women, Olympians and veterans. The club is known not only in Britain, but throughout Europe. That is an amazing feat, of which not only Truronians (as they are called) are proud. The club is truly a community, and some of that good feeling comes through in this publication.

There are many volumes about fencing. I have contributed one of them. Some are written by ex-internationals, who have often forgotten what it is like to learn from the beginning. A number of excellent books have appeared in foreign languages, but sadly their translators have not always done them a service. (My own book, when translated into Italian, had to be quickly amended when an Italian friend informed my publishers that in his language 'to lunge' was similar to 'to fall over', and people were falling over regularly from first page to last.) Other manuals have been written by club fencers who fancy themselves as authors, but don't really deeply understand the sport. *From Last to First* is the real deal, a book that is written by someone who really knows the sport in depth and knows how to teach and coach it, while working closely with Daniela Norris, an experienced author, who has ensured that the chapters read well, and are structured, clear and entertaining.

The biographical notes (see 'About the authors') mention that Jon was for many years a professional musician, a flamenco guitarist. The Spanish word *flamenco* is said to be a derivative of *flama*, meaning fire or flame, so that the word *flamenco* came to be used for 'fiery behaviour'. I like to think that in Jon's case it can be translated as 'passion', as it is his passion for the sport that makes him stand out as a coach. One doesn't want just to learn; one wants to be inspired.

A final thought, less about the book than my feeling when I come across Jon's students in competition: they seem to have so much fun doing it! Young fencers learn that two contestants, as they line up against each other to fence, will be told by their referee, "En garde!" Before they begin to fence, they must prepare above all to defend themselves. In Jon's students' case, the referee might well amend his or her instruction to "Prepare to attack!"

Richard Cohen is the former publishing director of Hutchinson and Hodder & Stoughton, the author of Chasing the Sun, By the Sword and How to Write Like Tolstoy, and the founder of Richard Cohen Books.

He was a visiting professor in creative writing at the University of Kingston-upon-Thames in London and for two years he was program director of the Cheltenham Festival of Literature.

Five times UK national sabre champion, Cohen was selected for the British Olympic fencing team in 1972, 1976, 1980 and 1984. He has written for the New York Times, the Wall Street Journal, the New York Times Book Review and most British quality newspapers.

Chapter 1

En garde

Welcome to fencing

Somehow you have stumbled upon the sport of fencing...

Maybe you know someone who fences, or perhaps you've seen some fencing on television or in a movie, and were inspired by the skill, power, speed and focus of this sport. Perhaps it is your daughter or son who wanted to try out fencing, somewhere between trying basketball, football and hockey. Or maybe fencing is something that always intrigued you and it is only now that the opportunity has come along. One way or another, congratulations on finding us, and welcome to the magical, competitive and rigorous world of this martial art – the Olympic sport of fencing.

For centuries, even millennia, people wielded swords as weapons of war. Swords made of iron first appeared around the twelfth century BC but did not become widespread until four centuries later. Holding a sword in your hand brings a very primal sensation of power, and many children are naturally attracted to the feeling of control and accomplishment that knowing how to hold and use a sword can bring.

Mastering the use of a sword is a highly technical skill – one that can help develop self-confidence, focus and precision in children and adults alike.

Children can start fencing at a young age, with some clubs offering fencing groups for participants as young as 5, and 'parent and child' groups at even younger ages. This does not necessarily mean they will become child prodigies, but simply that they will be exposed to the fencing environment at an early age, and perhaps might fall in love with it. Conversely, many successful fencers have started their journey in the sport later; so don't write off your child's (or your!) chances.

Fencing encourages physical and mental balance, focus, analytical skills, discipline and thinking ahead. It helps to develop the frontal lobe of the brain – an advantage for hyperactive children and for those who need help with concentration. Fencing is a uniquely demanding sport in the way that it demands technical, physical, tactical and psychological prowess, and the benefits to the individual are enormous.

The eighteenth-century Italian school of fencing, developed during the Renaissance, is credited as the origin of modern fencing, and the French school built on and further developed the Italian techniques. Historical references to fencing schools date back to the twelfth century, but it is only in the mid-eighteenth century that a shift towards fencing as a sport happened. This was led by Domenico Angelo, who established a fencing academy called Angelo's School of Arms, in Carlisle House, Soho, London in 1763. Domenico Angelo taught the aristocracy the fashionable art of swordsmanship.

As a fencing instructor to the Royal Family, he – and his sons after him – dominated European fencing for nearly a century. He established the essential rules of posture and footwork and was the first fencing master to point out the health and sporting benefits of fencing, more than its use as a form of combat. As a result of this changing perspective, fencing slowly evolved from an art of war into a sport.

While there are various theories and traditions about the starting weapon (most often, especially in Western Europe, children started with foil, before having the choice to move on to épée or sabre later, or to continue with the foil), it is now widely accepted that under the age of 6, and before children have enough discipline and self-control to ensure safety, and the strength to use a metal sword, it is recommended that they start with a foam or plastic weapon.

Daniela says:

> Watching the joy in the eyes of my boys the first time they were allowed to hold a real fencing sword and learned some basic skills was exhilarating. My older boy had issues with concentration at school – as a young child he was unable to do repetitive tasks required of him and needed to move from activity to activity all the time – nothing held his interest for an extended period. Fencing was life-changing for him. Very quickly, the benefits of his weekly practice were evident, and he wanted to train two and three times a week. There was no one club near us that provided that – so I found myself driving him to a different town so that he could train more

often. But it was totally worth it!

Jon says:

It is important early on to get a balance between training hard and overspecialising. Specialisation is not desirable at a young age. Motivation and commitment should come from the fencer, not the parent, but once they have committed to a program, the fencer should learn the importance of consistent training. A good coach will know how hard to push a young fencer, and when rest is required. Young fencers with potential often have other demands on them, academic or sporting (or both), and it is important that they keep their love of the sport and are self-motivated.

You might be worried that fencing is an expensive sport – it can be, but this can be managed intelligently. It is not necessary to rush out and buy costly fencing equipment right away. The first thing you might want to invest in is a modestly priced fencing glove, which is a personal item and can be more hygienic to own rather than borrow! It is also easy to carry around and to bring to training and will give your child a feeling of investment in the sport right away. The gloves for foil, épée and sabre are different, so make sure your child has decided which weapon they intend to train with, before you buy the glove. And of course, consult your child's coach.

It's better to spend a little time in the sport, and for the fencer to settle on which of the three disciplines appeals most, before buying a full set of kit. Most of the safety equipment (except for the mask) is uniform across the weapons, but some items are specialist, and it's easy to waste money needlessly with hasty purchases!

A second worthy investment is a mask – these are different for foil, épée and sabre, so make sure you know what you're buying. Excellent-condition masks can often be obtained second-hand for far less than a new item. Obviously, your child's head will grow over the coming years and masks come in different sizes, so a pre-loved mask can be a good idea. Later, when your child starts serious competitions, you'll be able to invest in a new mask, and their size might have changed in the meantime too.

Many clubs lend or hire out the more expensive equipment such as fencing jackets, breeches, lamés, plastrons, chest protectors and swords. You can often buy all these items second-hand through your club or through online forums. There are also additional items of equipment, such as body and mask wires (depending on the weapon) – it is best not to buy these second-hand, because they might not be in perfect working condition.

There are different protective levels of equipment (marked as 350N or 800N, which describes the force it will withstand; N = newtons, a unit of force). 800N items are required for higher-level competitions, and cost more. Your coach will advise you which level of protection is required for each item. We would always recommend an 800N plastron (the layer of protection under the jacket).

Here is a rough estimate of what beginner fencing equipment will cost for a child, if buying new from a reputable company (remember, you can always start with second-hand and then upgrade if and when necessary):

Glove $25–$60/£20–£50 (more expensive for sabre, as the glove is conductive)

Mask $100–$250/£80–£200 (more expensive for sabre, as the mask is conductive)

Breeches $60–$120/£50–£100 (and more for 800N, which provide more protection when competing at higher levels)

Fencing jacket $100–$200/£80–£160 (and more for 800N)

Plastron $50–$100/£40–£80 (800N obligatory when fencing with full-size weapons – normally age 13 upwards)

Chest guard/protector $25–$40/£20–£35

Electric jacket ('lamé') $100–$300/£80–£240 (for foil and sabre – no lamé required for épée!)

Body wire $15–$25/£12–£20

Mask wire $5–$10/£4–£8

Fencing bag to carry equipment $50–$240/£40–£190 (for a large-size bag with wheels)

Specialist fencing shoes and socks are also available. Fencing shoes aren't really necessary at the beginning, but as training becomes more intensive, and the fencer begins competing, they are worth considering. The special areas of support, protection against wear, grip, shock absorption and profile of fencing shoes are useful. That said, particularly in épée fencing (due to the nature of épée footwork), even top fencers sometimes choose to wear alternatives such as handball or squash shoes.

In the first stages of your child's fencing, consider borrowing, hiring or buying second-hand equipment; this way your financial investment will not be overwhelming and as your child progresses and invests more of their time and effort in the sport – and grows physically – you can slowly invest more and more, perhaps buying pieces of equipment as presents for birthdays and special occasions. The investment does not need to be immediate, and many items will last a very long time!

Weapon sizes also change as your child grows – different countries have slightly different rules for the use of blade sizes. Although it will vary according to your fencing federation, often up to 9-years-of-age a size 0 blade is used, then a size 2 (épée/sabre) or size 3 (foil) from age 10 to 13, and ultimately a standard-size 5 from the age of 14.

The official language of the sport of fencing is traditionally French. Many countries around the world still use the French terms for many fencing actions and for refereeing and for the terminology of the training and competing area.

Therefore, the fencing training hall is called a *salle* (pronounced SALL) and the field of play is called a *piste*. However, in the USA, the term 'strip' is used for *piste*, and many of the French words for different fencing movements and positions have been replaced with English alternatives.

We explain the basic rules of fencing in more detail in the next chapter, but for now you should know that there are three modern fencing weapons – foil, épée and sabre – each of which has different rules, techniques and target areas.

Now, equipped with this basic information, you are in the en garde position and ready to start!

Chapter 2

Ready

Some basic fencing rules

In this chapter we're going to introduce you to the basic rules of the three weapons of modern fencing (foil, épée and sabre) and explain a little about how the scoring equipment and refereeing works.

As a spectator, your first impression of fencing may well be quite a confusing experience. When the sheer speed of the sport is combined with rules of attack and defence, the electronic scoring equipment with variously coloured lights flashing on and off, and often, in competition, the use of French terms by referees, the newcomer can quickly conclude that fencing is obscure and difficult to follow.

Although this is indeed partly true, it has been exacerbated by the fact that fencing as a sport has traditionally been ineffective at explaining and presenting itself to the non-fencing audience.

While in recent years huge strides have been made in this regard at world level, new fencers or fencing parents may still initially find this to be a strange, and possibly daunting, world.

The good news is that, with the explanation of a few basic rules and a rudimentary understanding of how the scoring equipment and refereeing work, anyone new to the sport can quickly and easily understand (and hopefully enjoy!) the experience of spectating, or indeed participating in, fencing. So here goes...

First, we need to remember that there are three different weapons in fencing (foil, épée and sabre), and that each has slightly different rules, tactics and techniques. Think of it in the same terms as tennis, badminton and squash: all three have similar aims and objectives, and some related skills, but each has its own individual characteristics, and varies in its speed, rules, technical requirements, tactics and so on. While two centuries ago the winner of a duel was determined by the first fencer to draw blood from their opponent, modern fencing weapons are linked up to electronic scoring equipment. At major world events they feature wireless technology and online systems with live scoring updates in real time. All three weapons are featured in the Olympic Games every 4 years, and in the World Fencing Championships in non-Olympic years. There are individual and team events for both men and women in each of the three weapons, giving a total of 12 Olympic and World Championship events.

When watching fencing, keep in mind which of the weapons is on show, and what the rules of that specific weapon are. Let's have a look at the differences between the three different swords used in the modern sport.

Épée

The épée is descended from the duelling rapier of the sixteenth and seventeenth centuries and is the heaviest of the three fencing weapons. The rapier in various forms was used as a duelling weapon and weapon of war for many hundreds of years, and over time evolved into the more stylised épée fencing.

The épée is a thrusting weapon with a spring-loaded tip, which requires 750 grams of pressure to register a valid hit. The target area is the whole body, from the toes to the top of the head! Épée has the simplest rules of the three weapons: whichever fencer hits first will score a point. If both fencers hit within 50 milliseconds of one another, both scoring lights are illuminated on the box, and each fencer is awarded a point.

The épée is a cagey and tactical weapon, requiring excellent planning and concentration, and the purists will tell you that it is the closest to 'real' duelling of any fencing. Épée is the most globally widespread of the three weapons, as it requires simpler and slightly cheaper equipment, and is more straightforward to introduce to newcomers.

Foil

The foil is descended from the training weapon for the eighteenth-century small-sword, which was used by swordsmen (and sometimes women) to train and improve their skills, and in many cases to prepare for one-on-one duelling.

The Foil is a thrusting weapon, so only the hits made with the point of the blade will count, and the target area is the torso, with the head, arms and legs being off-target. The target includes the groin and the back. Throughout the late eighteenth and nineteenth century foil fencing became more focused on elegance and excellent technique, and so developed into the modern sport we see today.

Foil has rules of attack and defence, which determine who is awarded a point when the two fencers hit each other at the same time. To summarise and simplify these rules, the fencer who begins to attack first has the priority. In this situation if the defender simply counter-attacks, and both fencers hit, the attacker is awarded the point by the referee. In practice, the attacker is the fencer who starts a forward movement threatening the opponent (of course the interpretation of what constitutes an attack has more subtlety than that, but this simple explanation is enough to get you started). Once an attack is established, the onus is on the defender to block the attack with a parry, hit the opponent's blade away with a beat or other blade action, or to make the attacker miss. Once the defender has managed to perform one of these actions, the priority then passes to them and they become the attacker. These rules of attack and defence only come into play if both fencers hit each other – if there's only one light on the scoring equipment then the referee has no need to make a decision.

It is worth remembering that the white off-target light is treated the same as an on-target light for the purposes of awarding priority; that is, if the attacker hits the opponent off-target, and the defender counter-attacks, then the off-target attack had priority and no hit is awarded.

Sabre

The sabre is descended from the cavalry sabre of the eighteenth and nineteenth century. It was originally a brutal cutting weapon, and has roots in Eastern Europe's light cavalry.

Sabre is unique in modern fencing in that it is the only weapon where touches with either the edge *or* the point of the blade are valid. Sabre originated as a cavalry weapon and so was traditionally used on horseback. The target area for sabre therefore is from the waist up, including the arms and the head. Any touch, however light, on the valid target will register a light for the scoring fencer. Touches below the waist are off-target, but do not register a light, and are ignored. Another unique feature of sabre fencing is that it is against the rules for a fencer to bring their rear foot in front of their leading foot – this 'running' movement is allowed in épée and foil, but in sabre is punished with a yellow card.

As with foil, sabre fencing features rules of attack and defence, with priority awarded to the fencer who begins their attack first. Sabre is the fastest and most explosive of the modern weapons and is at once the most exciting to watch for non-fencers and the hardest to follow, partly because of its sheer speed.

Many people only ever fence one weapon, but some try two or all three weapons before settling on their favourite. Generally, fencers either specialise, or at least focus more on one discipline. It is very rare in the modern era for high-level fencers to switch weapons, although it is not unheard of. Many clubs will specialise in one or two of the weapons, as it can be logistically difficult and expensive to operate two or three different training groups, or to employ specialist coaches in different disciplines, especially in a high-performance club. If your club trains in more than one weapon, then let your child have a go at all the options available. Often one weapon will either suit their mentality or character better, or they'll simply enjoy one more than another, and so be more motivated to train and to stay with the sport in the long term.

As in many combat sports, left-handed fencers have a slight statistical advantage, with around 25 per cent of leading world-level fencers being left-handed, versus approximately 10 per cent of the population. There is an argument that this is because left-handers are obviously far more used to fencing right-handers, and right-handers are forced to deal with more unfamiliar angles and openings when they fence left-handers. However, it is difficult to justify this at the very highest level, when all the leading fencers have outstanding technique and adaptability.

Jon says:

I believe that neither left- or right-handedness is an indicator of ability to succeed or fail at the top level – there are numerous other factors, which are far more influential. It is worth considering that this statistic is likely to be an outcome of young left-handers experiencing proportionately more early success, and therefore a greater proportion of left-handers (and their parents!) being inspired and motivated to train hard and commit to the sport. This quite logically indicates that the outcome of commitment to training over a long period of time is the real reason these athletes become successful.

Fencing is an extremely safe sport, due to the high standard of safety equipment used at all levels of the sport. A fencer's protective uniform includes:

A plastron (a half-jacket covering the sword-arm side of the body)
A jacket, which covers the body, arms and groin
A mask made of steel mesh, firmly secured with a strap on the back, to protect the face, neck and head
A glove to protect the sword hand and overlap the jacket to prevent the opponent's sword going up the jacket sleeve
Fencing trousers, called 'breeches' in the UK or 'knickers' in the USA, which end just below the knee
Long socks (or 'stockings' in the USA)
For women, a mandatory plastic chest protector under the jacket; some male fencers also choose to wear a chest protector, and it is common for young fencers of both sexes to wear them

The protective clothing is made of material resistant to between 350 and 800 newtons of force, depending on the level of competition. Due to the quality of the safety equipment, and the discipline and regulations in the training and competition environment, fencing is statistically far safer than almost any other sport that you or your child would be likely to try.

When watching fencing you will notice that there is a scoring box which lights up when the competing fencers touch one another with their fencing swords. When a fencer scores a point on the valid target, the light on their side of the box will light up (usually a red light for the fencer on the left and a green light for the fencer on the right). Foil is unique among the three weapons in that, when a fencer hits off-target, a white light is illuminated on the scoring box – in the other weapons non-valid hits simply don't register.

You will also notice that there is a referee in charge of the match and awarding the hits, or touches, to the fencers. At world level, referees officiate in French (see glossary of fencing terms for a list of French fencing words). At domestic level, referees often officiate in the home language, but French is sometimes used. Referees use hand signals to indicate who has been awarded the hit (and why the hit was awarded) or to clarify other decisions.

The fencers compete on a playing area called a 'piste' in Europe, or 'strip' in the USA. The piste is 14 metres long and between 1.5 and 2 metres wide. Fencers must stay in the playing area. Leaving the side of the piste, even with just one foot, will result in the referee calling halt and giving a 1-metre penalty to the fencer leaving the piste. If a fencer crosses the rear boundary of the piste with *both* feet, the referee will call halt, and a point will be awarded to the opponent. At serious competitions, and in many permanent fencing venues, the fencing pistes are made of conductive aluminium panels, in order that any touches on the floor are short-circuited and won't register on the scoring equipment.

Referees can award yellow and red cards for breaches of the rules. A yellow card is awarded for a range of relatively minor offences (for example, coming on to the piste with malfunctioning equipment). A red card can be awarded for more serious offences *or* for a second and further minor offences. A yellow card is a warning card, whereas a red card results in a free point for the opponent. In rare cases of extreme unsporting behaviour, a black card is issued, which results in disqualification and can in some cases lead to a ban from competition for a time.

The usual format of competitions is to have pools or groups of five to seven competitors fencing each other in matches up to 5 hits. From these preliminary rounds, or 'pools', seedings are created, with the fencers who obtained the best pool results seeded at the top of the draw, down to the fencers who had the weakest pool results at the bottom of the draw.

The next stage of competition is called the 'direct elimination' (or DE for short). The higher seeds will then be drawn against lower seeds, and will fence an elimination match, with the winner progressing to the next round. There are various different event formats, especially in younger age-groups, with multiple rounds of pools, or 'repechage' elimination matches, which give losers of elimination fights a chance to fight their way back into the main draw. At world level, the simple 'elimination' system is used.

Elimination matches are generally fenced up to 10 hits in youth events, and 15 hits for fencers aged 14 and over. The age cut-offs and target scores vary slightly from country to country in youth competitions, but at world level all pool matches are up to 5 hits, and elimination matches to 15. In épée and foil there is a time limit of 3 minutes for a pool match, and three periods of 3 minutes (with a 1-minute break between each period) for an elimination match. Sabre bouts are over so quickly that time never plays a part – in matches to 10 hits, sabre fencers will take a 1-minute break when one competitor reaches 5, and in matches to 15 hits when one competitor reaches 8. During the minute breaks, coaches can discuss strategy and tactics with the fencers, while the fencer can rehydrate, rest for a few seconds and consider their plans for the next period of the match. It is very common to see a change of tactics and momentum after a

1-minute break.

If time runs out in a foil or épée bout, whoever is leading wins the match. If scores are tied, an additional minute is fenced, with one fencer being awarded 'priority' at random. In the additional minute the next hit will win the match, or if no hit is scored then the fencer with priority wins. Fencers progress through elimination matches to quarter-finals, semi-finals and a final to decide the competition winner. Losing semi-finalists are normally placed in equal third place *except* at the Olympic Games, where a bronze medal match is fenced.

Finally, when watching fencing as a newcomer, don't be shy of asking people around to explain rules or to help you understand referees' decisions. There are often experienced fencers, coaches or clued-up fencing parents watching who would be more than happy to explain what's going on! Do not approach referees during bouts, but most referees will be happy to explain rules when they're free in-between rounds. It's also a good idea to find good-quality fencing matches online, and spend some time watching these matches (sometimes even in slow motion, as it will be easier to see the actions) in order to familiarise yourself with the rules of attack and defence, the lights on the scoring apparatus, referees' hand signals, and the influence of the time limit in foil and épée.

Remembering some of the basic rules, spending a little time watching online and not being shy to ask questions will mean that in no time at all you'll start to understand what's happening on the piste, and be familiar with rules and competition formats.

Chapter 3

Fence

How does fencing work?

Fencing is a unique sport, with a complex and ancient history, and a set of technical, physical and mental requirements which are extraordinarily difficult and take years to master. Although in some countries such as France, Italy and Hungary it is regarded as a much more mainstream sport, it still raises quite a few eyebrows when discussed in the USA and UK, and many other places around the world.

Italian fencing master Domenico Angelo, instructor to the British and French aristocracy and many of the upper classes of eighteenth-century London and Paris, believed fencing helped to develop health, poise and grace. As a result of this insight, and the influence of his work and of great fencing masters of the time, swordplay gradually began to transform from an important element of warfare into a more stylised art form, and ultimately a competitive sport. The timing of this evolution of swordplay went in parallel with the proliferation of new and improving military weapon technologies, and industrial mass production of arms and gunpowder, which ultimately rendered the sword useless as a weapon of war. Ironically, this was the making of fencing as a sport, initially for the aristocratic classes, and later as an Olympic sport for all.

In his classic book *The School of Fencing*, first published in 1763, Angelo begins by explaining that: "When the Goths had introduced the art of single combat, the art of defence became a necessary study: it was confined to certain rules, and academies were instituted to train up youth in the practice of them." In the word 'defence' lies the origin of the word 'fencing'.

While most of us living in the Western world don't find it necessary to be trained in the art of single combat, the centuries of tradition and the history of swordplay and other martial arts still hold a fascination for many people, and there is a perception of it as a more honourable style of combat than the use of firearms.

Today's fencing masters stand on the shoulders of giants, who transformed swordplay from brutal combat to technical and tactical wizardry, and many of whose techniques are employed in modern fencing hundreds of years later; today's fencing students walk the same paths that have been walked by many before them, in learning, training and falling in love with the beauty of fencing. While fencing has been modernised by the introduction of electric equipment and modern fencing weapons, the principles of wielding a sword remain the same: precision, focus, control, technique, power and a host of physical and mental abilities. Most of these can be taught, learned, practised, honed and mastered over time – but there are no shortcuts.

Fencing is a sport requiring a range of different types of training:

and women in all three disciplines of foil, épée and sabre. The psychology of individual and team fencing is not identical, and each requires a different approach strategically and mentally. It would be wrong to say that there is a specific mindset which works for all fencers, as all athletes are individuals and will find individual ways to deal with commitment, disappointment, maintaining motivation, injury, performing under pressure and so on. However, there are clearly common denominators shared by top fencers, and many leading athletes in other sports, which are worth considering.

In the early days, motivation is key – the young fencer needs to be engaged and passionate about the sport. If they are to become successful in the future, they will need to commit for a long period of time to a tough training regime. Differentiating between motivation and commitment is very important. A young fencer will be motivated and fascinated by their new sport, but there will come a time when they need to go beyond motivation and understand commitment.

Jon says:

Just before the London Olympic Games in 2012, I had a fascinating one-to-one meeting with the great sports psychologist and clinical psychiatrist, Dr Steve Peters. Dr Peters was the psychologist for British Cycling, one of the world's most successful sports teams, and is the author of the best-seller *The Chimp Paradox*. He described his view of the difference between motivation and commitment to me as follows:

"Imagine a brain surgeon embarking on a risky operation. The surgeon gets halfway through the potentially life-saving surgery and gets tired and fed up. He or she isn't motivated any more. But they have committed to carrying out the surgery, and so they continue, and finish the operation successfully, saving the patient's life. There was no guarantee of a successful operation if the surgeon completed the procedure, but there was a guarantee of failure if they didn't. Sometimes as an athlete your motivation will waver, you won't want to get up early and go to the gym, you won't want to put on your sweaty kit in a cold sports hall and fence one more training match. But you have committed: you *must* do it. There are no guarantees of success if you do, but there is a guarantee of failure if you don't."

Of course, there are many reasons to practise fencing: enthusiasm and fascination for the sport, the fun and social aspect of belonging to any sports club or any group of like-minded people with a shared interest, the desire for improvement, for fitness, for an escape from pressures of work or school. But for the serious competitor, once they have decided to embark on the long and arduous quest to become a top-class fencer, long-term commitment must be maintained when these motivations waver, or some of them even disappear.

Fencing is very much an 'in the moment' sport – it requires exceptionally high focus for concentrated periods of time, bursts of explosive physical energy, technical 'muscle memory' built through frequent and intensive training and skills repetition, the ability to analyse and outwit an opponent, patience combined with opportunism, the cunning to feed false information, creativity combined with discipline, and to win at the top level sometimes a modicum of luck is helpful!

After the very early stages, if your child is not willing and able to train at least twice a week, and at a higher youth level three to four times a week, going on to four to five times a week plus fitness and other training as they start to compete nationally, and if you are not willing to put in the time and commitment that getting them to and from training and competitions requires, they will be at a huge disadvantage.

Reduced training volume has a cumulative effect. To illustrate this, Jon repeats the following conversation with every generation of young fencers when they start to commit to the sport and move up to higher-intensity training:

> **Jon:** If you talked a little less, or got ready to train a little faster, or were always on time, would you be able to fit in three extra training matches into your session?
>
> **Fencers:** Yes. (All young fencers *always* reply yes to this!)
>
> **Jon:** So, if you train three or four times a week, you could manage perhaps 10 more matches a week. You train about 40–45 weeks a year, so that's about 400 matches a year… In 10 years when you're trying to qualify for the Olympic Games you will have missed 4000 matches. Who is more likely to win? You? Or your opponent who didn't miss the 4000 matches?

The impact of this conversation on young fencers is generally very strong, and it's worth repeating it from time to time, but it's also worth parents recognising the cumulative effect of missed sessions, or arriving late, or leaving early.

Many fencers and their parents discover at quite an early stage of their fencing journey that, unlike football, soccer, basketball and tennis, there isn't much money in fencing. Even if your child becomes a successful young fencer, it is highly likely that you'll still need to fund quite a lot of the costs of them practising this unique sport. Later on, at senior level, many countries have funded programs, but this is not uniform across nations. Some high-level competitions have small amounts of prize money, and some top athletes are lucky enough to find a commercial sponsor to support them. However, there are also some fencers in the world top 50 who struggle to pay for their sport, and who work part-time, or coach or fundraise so that they can fulfil a serious program of competitions and training and represent their country at World Cups, Grand Prix and major championships.

There are several historic and structural reasons for this financial disparity with many other sports:

1. Fencing has struggled to shake off its image as an elite sport with overly complicated rules. While it is true that perhaps the rules of fencing are not immediately obvious, if one is willing to dedicate a little time to understanding them, they become very clear. The rules are no more complex than the rules of gridiron, cricket or rugby, but of course these sports have a long tradition of enormous participation and are in the public consciousness. Relatively low participation, compared to huge global sports, means relatively low revenues into the sport.

2. While in a more mainstream sport like football/soccer the World Cup attracts many millions of spectators and viewers, a World Fencing Championship final may only attract a few thousand spectators. Big commercial sponsors are therefore far less interested in investing in fencers and fencing than in sports where their brand or product will get exponentially greater exposure. A sport which attracts many millions of viewers will also command huge sums of money for broadcasting rights of events, matches and championships, and fencing doesn't have this advantage.

3. A large amount of the money in many sports comes from equipment and clothing manufacturers. Tennis, golf, track and field and many others all have a huge base of participation, and manufacturers of equipment and clothing in sports of this type will gain great commercial benefit in promoting their brands by supporting events or individuals. Clothing in many of these sports has become day-to-day fashion wear, and the products are commercially very successful independently from the

active participants in their sports. Fencing has a number of disadvantages in this area – as with general commercial sponsorship mentioned above, brands will gain limited exposure as the sport has relatively low participation and coverage; and additionally, fencing clothing is not suitable for day-to-day fashion wear, meaning that manufacturers are limited to selling products to active participants.

4. Finally, that elitist image mentioned earlier sometimes leads potential supporters and sponsors to think that fencers don't *need* financial backing. The 'elitist' view of fencing doesn't hold true in global terms: programs around the world are aiming to recruit youngsters from all backgrounds, and to help them reach their medal-winning potential. The reality is that many, many fencers come from ordinary backgrounds, not from the ranks of the super-rich, and struggle to support themselves and their training and competition costs. The message that fencing should and can be for anyone, whatever their background, needs to be broadcast more effectively by the global fencing community.

Although the commercial fencing environment has begun to evolve slowly in recent years, with the process of globalisation of the sport, there is still no revenue for broadcast rights, and very little temptation for big commercial sponsors to throw large sums of money into the pot. For the top athletes there can, however, still be some significant benefits. These may be in the form of university scholarships, lower-level sponsorships from kit manufacturers, prize money, support through government-funded national programs, or support from various international or national funds, but fencing is not a sport that will bring in millions for an individual high performer.

Aside from the hard benefits, fencing develops individuals

who can think for themselves, take calculated risks, understand the importance of work ethic, dedication to excellence, professionalism and commitment, deal with adversity and maintain focus under pressure – all characteristics which any employer, college or university would value.

When embarking on the path to becoming a top-level fencer, the holistic benefits to the individual, and the personal characteristics it can develop, should all be considerations which exceed that of merely gaining a big pay packet.

Chapter 4

Environment and culture

Researching the best club and coach for your child

Fencing is a sport where good-quality early grounding plays an important part in long-term success. While of course it is not impossible to overcome problems with hand or footwork technique, distance, timing, or a myriad of other areas, which can result from poor early coaching, any coach will tell you that it is far easier to train new good habits into a fencer than it is to break old bad habits. As you might expect, fencing clubs vary greatly in their goals, modus operandi and quality of delivery. Some fencing clubs are more competitive than others, and focused on developing performance fencers, some are largely recreational participation clubs, and some combine both these aspects of the sport. Different coaches will inevitably have different approaches to training young fencers, and indeed to working with top-level fencers too. One of the beauties of fencing is that there is more than one good route to achieving your goals, and there are many recognised technical and tactical schools and styles. However, while there are many different approaches which can work, there are also infinite ways to get it wrong!

Naturally, just as in any profession or walk of life, the level, motivation and style of coaches varies greatly. Be aware that, although a good level of qualification has its merits, it is not necessarily a clear indicator of a coach's success in their field, or their coaching culture and suitability for your child. Many less experienced, less well-qualified coaches may be doing a great job, so do not discount someone just because they don't have a large roster of top-level results, and equally don't be too dazzled by a glowing CV of medals!

First and foremost, you know your child best, and it is vital that both you and they feel comfortable, inspired and engaged at the club where they are training, and that there is a positive feeling from the coaching team. It is perfectly reasonable to try more than one club before you make a choice – listening to how your child feels after a session, or several sessions, at a certain club is very important. While one coach can be right for some young fencers, they may not be the perfect coach for others, and this will depend greatly on their coaching pedagogy, their personality, the training environment and the approach and attitude of other fencers in the classes. Most clubs will run introductory lessons or courses, and this is a great way to get a feel of the club, without making any long-term commitment, and of course it will allow your child to learn in a less intimidating environment alongside other beginners and to decide if fencing is for them.

The following are all positive signs to look out for in a fencing club, but are not always indicators by themselves that everything is right:

- Friendly but disciplined classes with a good structure: Most classes for young fencers will start with some elements of physical warm-up, tactical or skill-based games, and/or athletic skills development. Classes may have a combination of technical and tactical fencing exercises or scenarios, blade-work exercises, general sparring (also called free-fencing or bouting). Some coaches focus more on imparting tactical 'game' knowledge at the start; others establish the technical basics early in training. Ultimately, both these elements are essential and good coaches will address both areas over the first few weeks and months.
- A welcoming atmosphere and good communication: In a successful and healthy club, the staff, parents and fencers will generally be welcoming to new fencing families (although of course not every parent and every fencer will always be having a good day!), and coaches will be keen to engage and answer questions that you may have. Be aware that coaches have sessions to run and fencers to supervise, so may not always have time to speak at length at the precise moment that suits you.
- A strong work ethic among the fencers and the staff: It is very important that the coaching team builds an environment where the fencers work hard and understand the need for commitment and focus. Well-structured and well-managed sessions run by a coaching team that is engaged and motivates the children will lead to positive outcomes for all.
- Good results at a high level by athletes at the club: If a club

consistently produces good national-level results over a long period of time with a variety of fencers, that can be an excellent indicator of their ability to provide your child with the tools to reach their potential. However, continuously good results by just one or two individuals in a large club might indicate that the coaching team is focused only on one or two high performers; and be aware that those high performers may not even have started their fencing at that club or that their results may be the exception rather than the rule.

- Exaggerated regional results are not an indicator of ability to coach to a high level! While it is absolutely a great idea to make a young fencer feel proud about winning a medal at a small regional or local event, and to report that achievement in glowing terms on the club website or in the local press, it is not necessarily relevant to the club's or coach's ability to perform at national or international level.

- Consistent solid results by a young or relatively inexperienced coach or coaching team are a good indicator that they're doing the right things, and a CV of long-term strong results by a more experienced coach or coaching team with many different fencers is obviously a very good sign.

- Speak to other parents about their experiences: Almost any parent is likely to be willing to talk at length about their own child! It's worth speaking to friendly parents about the coaches, the club, their own experiences in training and competition and what their child's goals in the sport are, how often they train and so on. A child who only trains once a week and fences for fun can't be expected to be scoring top-class national results, so put the parents' experience and the child's progress in context.

- And finally, if the majority of parents seem happy and

impressed with the club and the environment, and pleased with their child's progress, don't give too much weight to one parent who isn't – pleasing most of the people most of the time is all any coach and club can hope for!

Daniela's story:

My son, Roman, has trained in four different clubs over a period of seven years.

His first club was a very small and friendly local French club where he started training at the age of 8 – it was a fun environment where the kids had enjoyed the sport but did not produce great results. Roman initially fenced foil, and training took place once a week in a gym that was converted into a fencing salle. While the sessions were enjoyable, and he really liked the coach, Roman really wanted to try sabre, which that club did not offer. After a short while it did not feel challenging for my son – he wanted more, and he also wanted to compete and win!

We moved on to training at another local club, slightly farther away, which offered sabre training – but again, only once a week, for one hour only. There were two other kids who were interested in competing, and together with my son they made a very small but good young squad, at the age of 10.

Roman managed to get some good results in the first few competitions he entered, and this motivated him to train more. Unfortunately, no extra sessions were offered at that club, and the other two competing boys were more interested in football than in fencing.

Hence the move to a third club – over the border in Geneva, Switzerland – where a great French coach trained a group of very motivated Swiss fencers three afternoons a week. This meant driving for half an hour, three times a week after school and hanging around for nearly two hours with my then-toddler, while the older boy, now 11 years old, was training. It didn't feel like a huge sacrifice on my part, as I saw how much my son loved training there, and I appreciated the coaching and the atmosphere at the club. But, after a while, I started wishing there was another solution, and perhaps a fresh approach.

That's when my son attended a summer fencing camp in the UK, in the small town of Truro in Cornwall. The week-long residential camp was hard work, but he loved the experience. The club had a history of producing excellent fencers, and the coaching team was friendly and had a lot of experience at the highest level. When we picked Roman up at the end of the week, the Head Coach Jon chatted to us and pointed out there was an option of boarding at Truro School, and training four times a week at the Truro Fencing Club on their high-performance program. Boarding school was not something I had ever considered before, but my son seemed to like the idea and so we considered the option. With some financial assistance and a lot of faith, we signed him up. 'If you don't like it, you can always come back home after a few months,' I said to my son, then just 12 years old. But he didn't want to come back – he loved the environment, worked hard, integrated into the club's squad and engaged well with the coaches. When he started training daily, with regular one-to-one lessons, sparring, fitness and footwork training and good sparring partners, the improvement in his understanding of the sport, his results and his increased motivation began to speak for themselves.

A year later, the whole family moved to Truro, Cornwall, and my son continued to attend Truro School, but no longer as a boarder. Still a part of Truro Fencing Club's intensive program, he has consistently improved and is still in love with the sport and his new-found club.

Many people asked me why I was willing to make the 'sacrifice' of moving for my son's fencing and I always answer: people move for many reasons – I saw this as an opportunity and not as a sacrifice. I'm sure we would not have moved were it an unpleasant town or financially prohibitive, but as life's circumstances unfolded we were lucky enough to be able to take this opportunity. Fencing has taken our family to places we would have never been to otherwise, on new adventures and experiences.

Jon's perspective:

Truro Fencing Club is one of the UK's leading sabre clubs. It has produced many national champions at age groups from U10 to senior level and is the only club ever to hold the British men's and women's Cadet, Junior and Senior British Sabre Championship titles simultaneously. In 2009 the club started a high-performance program and has gone on to produce medal-winning performances at European and Junior World Cup level. Despite being in a relatively rural small town of 18,000 people, the club competes with some of the best around the world due to a culture of hard work, a fierce club loyalty, high-quality coaching and passion for the sport. Completely inadvertently the club began attracting young fencers from around the UK and internationally to relocate there for periods of time ranging from a couple of months to years. A strong and growing partnership with Truro School created the opportunity for younger fencers to come to Truro, board at the school, have an excellent academic experience and train at a high level. During our annual summer training camp, I spotted a young fencer from France working especially hard. He had a number of technical problems to address, and was frustrated with himself for not doing better, but he had a huge amount of fight, a good tactical brain and excellent timing. When his parents came to pick him up at the end of the week, we got talking and I mentioned that if Roman was interested in training with us more, he would be welcome, and I pointed his parents in the direction of the school boarding/fencing program. Within months Roman had joined us. He integrated into the club quickly, making friends and working very hard. Intensive technical and footwork training quickly brought improvement, and his results reflected that. When he returned to France to compete in age-group events, his peers (and their parents) were astonished at his progress over a relatively short time, and he returned with renewed motivation. Roman is now an established part of the club and its youth success, and his progress continues. Although he has a long way to go, his potential is very high, and he has high hopes for the future.

In Roman's case we encountered few obstacles in integrating him into our system – his English is fluent, he is a sociable and hard-working young fencer and he understood that he needed to make some changes. We have been lucky enough to have fencers come to us for varying lengths of time from Japan, Singapore, Germany, Spain, Hong Kong, France and elsewhere, as well as the UK, and one of the proudest moments of my coaching career was when, at the Junior World Championships, there were fencers who had trained in Truro competing for the national teams of Germany, Spain and Japan, as well as Great Britain!

It is worth mentioning that as a club, we have also had fencers leave our environment and go to train elsewhere. Because we have experienced both sides of this situation, we recognise that it is important for the parents and the fencer to handle this sensitively. Coaches, as well as parents, invest a great deal of time and effort in developing young fencers, and of course when they 'lose' a fencer it has an impact on them, possibly financially, and in terms of their training sessions, and sometimes emotionally. As a young coach I was very upset to lose one of my leading fencers, but as one gains more experience of both coaching and life, it becomes easier to see the bigger picture.

As always, communication is key. Speak with the coach and explain the reasons why you are moving; ask the coach of the new club to get in touch and communicate with the original coach about the fencer and their training; discuss the transition period; be clear how grateful you are for the work the coach has done to date; and, if necessary, keep the door open to return in the future. All these steps will serve to make the transition easier. Finally, be aware that it can also be an emotional decision for the fencer, and the fencer's clubmates, and it may take a little time to integrate into a new environment.

If you find a good, well-run club with a capable coach or coaching team, then stick with them for a period of time, but equally if you have choice, then shop around at first and find the environment that seems to work best for your child.

Chapter 5

. Dos and don'ts

How to support your young fencer

As a parent, it is often difficult to know how to support your child in and around the training and competition environments. Both these arenas can be unfamiliar and sometimes daunting territory, and of course they can vary from club to club and from competition to competition. However, even in a highly pressurised sports environment, there are some simple 'dos and don'ts' which will really help you and your child to get the most from the sport of fencing, and enable them to flourish and reach their potential as fencers, athletes and individuals.

Once again, communication with your child's coach is essential to getting this all-important area of your child's fencing life right. Some coaches will prefer different levels of involvement from parents, and most will be happy to discuss their perspective with you. Some may even have rules or guidelines or a Code of Conduct that they would like parents to adhere to. View this as a positive and professional modus operandi, not as a criticism of your parenting! If you are confident that the coach and club are providing a professional and productive environment, and that they are doing a good job in training your child, then you should respect their rules of engagement and the level of parental involvement which they expect.

Training

Coaches are, of course, present at all your child's training sessions, and your direct support during training will not be necessary, or probably even desirable. It is a good idea to let your child 'own' their fencing – let them feel it's their own hobby (or passion, or sometimes obsession!) rather than yours. Your support in the training arena should come in the most prosaic and practical of ways: making sure they get to and from training on time, that they have a chance to fuel up with good food and plentiful hydration both before and after training, that they have access to the equipment they need, and that they are engaged and interested in what they're doing. Some children will be shy and may find their first few sessions a bit daunting. Encouragement and support, rather than compelling them to attend, will usually be more effective in the long run. Others, of course, will be more outgoing and confident and you won't face any problems in getting started.

In the early days it may help your child if you stay to watch their session, but it's a good idea to gradually disengage from them, and to give them more and more space to grow and assume responsibility for their training. Remember, all children are different, and their biological, emotional and chronological ages are not always in sync. Make sure that any support you give is appropriate, and is adding to, not detracting from, your child's experience of training. Leave coaching advice to the coaches and confine yourself to encouragement and positive reinforcement!

Feel free to ask your child how their training session went, and what they were working on – but if they don't want to talk about it in depth, don't pressure them.

Don't criticise if they didn't win matches or they struggled with an exercise or a technique. Fencing is a complex and challenging sport, and the skills are not quickly and easily acquired. The fencers who grasp some basic techniques immediately and win their early training matches are not always those who go on to long-term success.

Consistent progression over time is the most important thing – progress in any skill isn't linear and there will always be ups and downs, so worrying about progress from one day to the next, and results at one-off competitions, is really not helpful! Your child should sometimes look back and realise how much they've learned and pat themselves on the back. This is not complacency: recognising achievements is an important motivator!

If they're upset or not enjoying training, and want to discuss it, try to engage rationally, not emotionally; if this is a recurring theme over time, or they feel it's difficult to discuss the problem, then it's an issue to raise with the coach.

Remember, the outcomes your child wants from the sport may not be the same as yours! Allow them space to develop their technical and tactical skills, confidence, and passion for the sport.

As a coach, Jon has developed many athletes from their earliest fencing days as young beginners into Cadet, Junior and Senior internationals:

The number one requirement for success in fencing is

commitment to good-quality training over a very long period of time. Without this, all other 'talents' or aptitudes are irrelevant. Therefore, any behaviour or action on the part of the fencer, parent or coach which detracts from a young fencer's love of fencing, or their likelihood to commit to training, will in turn detract from that fencer's chances of long-term success.

Fencers are very lucky in that their training is interesting, varied and challenging. Training in some sports can be a gruelling test of mental endurance, grinding through repetitive sessions. In fencing, there are sessions for technical and tactical training in groups, one-to-one training with a coach, competitive matches in the club environment, footwork sessions, games for athletic development, and strength and conditioning programs, and of course mental training. Sometimes a fencer will find training tough, competition outcomes disappointing and upsetting, and pressure and nerves difficult to deal with, but it will rarely be boring! The parents' job is to add to the positives, not the negatives, and ensure that in the final analysis the fencer retains and develops their love of the sport.

Competitions

Coaches regularly attend competitions to support their athletes, watch the progress, prepare and motivate them, offer advice, and of course to network and keep their finger on the pulse of their sport and their profession.

There will, however, be occasions when a coach cannot attend, or may have a large number of athletes to take care of at an event and cannot devote a great deal of time to your child. In this situation it is important to allow the fencer space to prepare themselves, and to an extent to look after themselves – do not try to become their temporary coach.

In the absence of a coach, of course, you might need to keep an eye on a younger and less-experienced fencer to make sure they're doing the right things (warming up before the event, kitting up and doing some practice matches in good time, going to the correct piste on time, hydrating and snacking through the day, and so on). As a youngster, it's easy to lose track of time, or forget something important, but first allow them the opportunity to get it right, or make a mistake, and then the learning process will be more effective.

Attending the appropriate events for your child's age and level of ability is essential in maintaining both their progress and their motivation. Of course, the coach will advise when your child is ready to compete, which events to do and what their goals are. Once your child has begun to build competition experience, many of their habits are set quite deeply and would be difficult to change, so it's a sensible idea to get the right habits developing early on. In the long term, this will stand them in good stead as they progress through the levels and age groups.

The most important things that you as a parent can influence will be the absolute basics: a nutritious meal the night before, a good night's sleep, a balanced breakfast on the day, arriving early, knowing your event time, having all the right kit in good working order, and of course remembering to enter the competition in advance!

Jon says:

The early days of competition are about learning *how* to compete: building excellent habits and routines, learning to enjoy and get the best out of yourself under pressure, and of course making mistakes and learning from them. A 'professional' mentality in warm-ups, nutrition and hydration, looking after kit, cooling down, and all the other basics of a competitor, go a long way to influencing the fencer's mentality on the piste.

Here are some things to think about before any competition:

- Make sure your child eats well in the evening before the competition – they might be too excited or too nervous to eat a proper breakfast in the morning, especially early on in their experience of competition fencing. A good balanced meal, and an eye on good hydration throughout the days before and on the day of the event, will make all the difference to the fencer's energy levels, and will positively affect concentration as well as their physical condition.

- Make sure they have all their kit in working order, and in their fencing bag, before they leave the house for the competition! This may be the day of the event, or of course the night or day before. It is important to note that you should help the fencer to become self-sufficient in looking after and packing their equipment, but of course you probably need to check up on a younger and less-experienced fencer to make sure the job has been done properly: forgetting a piece of equipment can prove to be an expensive mistake. A checklist of items can be a good idea (all the clothing and fencing kit required, as well as any other items, such as energy drinks and snacks, a change of clothes, a towel). At first, you should make this task a joint effort – checking and testing kit and packing their kit bag together – and as they learn the ropes, you can let them take over more responsibility, and just check back on them to make sure. If you want to learn more about testing equipment, again speak to the coach. If you or your child are handy people, you could consider doing a basic armourer's course to learn how equipment works, is maintained and repaired. Having these skills can save you a lot of money in the long run. Some clubs have a volunteer or part-time club armourer who can carry out repairs for a small charge. It's also worth noting that each of the three different weapons in fencing has slightly different equipment and testing requirements.

- If you're travelling far to your event, it is a good idea to try to get to the area of the venue at a reasonable time the night before. A good night's sleep is an important factor in optimal performance. Checking your travel time in advance, spending a few minutes researching places to eat, and the proximity and directions of your accommodation to the competition venue, can take away stress and make everything go smoothly. It can be extremely stressful for both child and parent (and coach!) to arrive late, get lost on the way, or not be able to find parking, so arriving early can be one of the best ways to ensure your child starts the day well.

- If possible, eat a good breakfast. A good balance of complex carbohydrates, protein and some fats, and of course good hydration, will start the fencer off on the right foot and help maintain energy throughout the day. Anything with too much saturated fat will result in energy not being released soon enough, and anything too sugary will mean an early spike in energy ('sugar rush'), followed by a rapid loss of energy ('sugar crash').

- Some coaches will arrange warm-up lessons or activities before the competition, so make sure you know the timetable for this. Even if this isn't the case, it's still advisable to get to the competition venue well before the 'check-in' time, and at least an hour before the beginning of the tournament. This will ensure that your child has time to find a good spot to base themselves and organise their kit, familiarise themselves with the environment, find out where the changing rooms and toilets are, and have plenty of time to warm up, get kitted up and be well-prepared for the start of the event.

If you don't know anyone at the competition, it is perfectly acceptable for your child to invite someone they don't know to have some warm-up matches with them. If their coach is present, then they will most likely help with this. If you're by yourself, then encourage your child to speak to other fencers – making friends is an important part of the sport – but try not to do it on their behalf, as it's also a great way to help develop their autonomy. One of the recurring themes when speaking to experienced fencers is their pleasure at having friends around the country, and indeed the world, whom they wouldn't have met were it not for their shared love of the sport. This applies to you, the parent, too! Speak to other parents, make new friends and develop an information and knowledge network.

If your child feels intimidated by the environment or by the other fencers, allow them some space to calm down; if the coach isn't present, encourage them to warm up intensively (which can dispel nervous energy), or have a drink and a think in a quiet corner. Don't try to give coaching advice! The most you should do is to ask what they've been working on in training; say that maybe they should try those things and try to fence using actions they've been working on. With time, competing will become second nature to them and they will thrive on the adrenalin rush that arriving at a competition venue can create.

If your child's coach is there, let them manage their fencers as they see fit: they've probably been in the same situation many times before, either as coach, competitor or both, and will understand far better than you how a young fencer is feeling and how to help them prepare for the competition. Keep your distance, but if you do think your child is struggling in terms of performance, nerves or anything else over a period of time (not just as a one-off), it's fine to mention that to the coach. Any more detailed conversations should be held away from the competition environment.

Remember, the early days of competition are about your

child experimenting with what works for them – be there for them if they need you but give them enough space to find their own 'zone' and develop their competition routine.

It is fine to offer a drink or snack to a fencer between matches but ask yourself first if you're invading your child's competition environment, and if they should just be left alone. Ultimately, the aim of early competition is to develop independent and self-reliant competitors, and habits that are established early on can last a lifetime. It's natural that you want your child to do well but don't indulge your own need to support and protect them – let them make mistakes and learn from them!

It is never fine to offer fencing advice – unless you are a very serious fencer or a coach yourself – and even then, you should consider that your child will have a different perspective on a parent's advice than on the advice of an independent coach. In general, the best solution for all is to leave their coach to do the job of giving fencing advice.

If the coach isn't at the piste for an important match, it's fine to let them know which piste and at what time your child is fencing, but do not expect them to be there if they have more than one fencer competing at the same time. Coaches will make their own judgements on which piste to be at, based on an enormous number of factors: the level of experience of the fencer; the relative likelihood of success in a particular match or competition; the value of the fencer's learning experience in having, or not having, a coach there. Some coaches might leave the fencer with the perceived best chance of success to their own devices until the later stages, confident they can negotiate the early rounds without feedback. Sometimes a coach will spend half a match with a fencer, and move on, having given some tactical feedback. Piste-side coaching styles also vary: some coaches are more vocal than others; some will give specific advice and others will just observe; some will encourage the fencer, and others will stay silent – the best coaches will use all of these strategies, depending on the circumstances and the individual fencer. Trust the coach to do the right thing, but if over time you feel that you're not getting fair treatment, then raise this away from the competition environment courteously and with an open mind. If the coach doesn't convince you that they have your fencer's best interest at heart, then ask yourself if you are at the right club or with the right coach.

Remember:

- The essential requirement for long-term success is that your child is committed to and motivated by training, so positive reinforcement and falling in love with the sport is key.
- Competitions are learning environments for young fencers and they should be encouraged to fence well, not just to win.
- Parents are taxi drivers, financiers, chefs, bag-packers and cheerleaders, but are usually not coaches. Leave fencing to the fencers and coaching to the coach!

Chapter 6

Positive communication

Getting along with your coach, fellow parents and club-mates

© Club d'escrime de Varces, France

Positive communication, especially with your child's coach, is an essential piece of the jigsaw in helping your child to get the best out of training, and in helping you to understand how they're progressing. You are far more likely to optimise their chances of improvement if you have a positive relationship built on good communication with your child's coach, and with other parents and fencers at the club.

If your child is lucky enough to have a committed and successful coach who cares about their athletes, then of course that coach is more likely to be very busy! And if your child continues training and starts competing, it is inevitable that you will see your child's coach often, at club sessions and perhaps at competitions, and will probably get to know them quite well. It is important to bear in mind, however, that the training session or competition environment is not necessarily the best place for anything other than brief communication – the coach is likely to be occupied with many other priorities, and they may not be able to give the time and consideration that you would want to your questions or concerns.

Other than coaching your child, coaches will usually have many other kids to work with (and probably adults, depending on the club and its structure). If your child goes to a smaller club with one coach, that coach will probably also need to do the club's administration and paperwork, make and receive phone calls and perhaps even clean behind the lockers once in a while! They probably care about the way their club looks and feels far more than the fencers who come to train there only a few times a week, and they will be putting in a lot of time and effort behind the scenes to make things run smoothly. All of that is on top of running the club's regular fencing sessions, giving private lessons, perhaps coaching in schools and colleges, and not forgetting the travel and coaching time put into competitions!

In a bigger club with multiple coaches, coaches usually share the club sessions and lessons, but they typically also have a larger number of fencers, simply resulting in multiple busy coaches. In a large club it is far more likely that there will be administrative and managerial support, and there will usually be a hierarchical system, with a Head Coach, and other staff responsible for different areas, levels of fencers and/or different weapons.

Coaches in a professional club environment will spend a great deal of their day at the club, and of course their evenings too when many of the sessions will take place. If your club is a smaller operation, coaches will often be working in schools or at other clubs at different times of the day. Competitions take place at weekends, and coaches will often be travelling to competitions and looking after their athletes at those events. Many coaches would say that they spend more time with their top fencers than with their own children – this is an inevitable price that an ambitious and motivated coach pays for their commitment to their athletes; how the coach's family feels about that is of course another question altogether! The workload, unsociable hours and amount of travel that many coaches will endure means that any time off is very valuable, so make sure that you respect their free time, and don't assume they are available to meet, reply to messages or emails, or speak to you on the phone at the drop of a hat.

Fencing coaches don't earn huge salaries – they are not up there with top lawyers, software engineers and fund managers, even if the demands on their time, specialist knowledge and attention to detail expected of them can sometimes exceed those of the professions above! Many fencing coaches are coaching part-time and have other jobs, and those who are full-time are rarely in their profession just to make money – they're usually passionate about their sport and their clubs, and they want to see their fencers reach their potential.

While you are the child's parent, and of course know them well, it is important to remember that the coach is the professional whose job it is to help develop your child's fencing abilities, as well as their attitude. Their perspective and experience will certainly be unlike yours, and they may perceive your child's progress, potential and place in the club very differently from you. The development of a young fencer is not linear, and the coach is likely to know best whether your child is on track or not, whether changes to training are needed, if you need to increase or reduce their training volume, or if the fencer needs any additional support technically, physically or psychologically. If you trust the coach, they have a good reputation, they coach other good athletes and run good sessions, then you should trust their professional opinion on these matters.

However busy they may be, a good coach will ultimately find the time to discuss their fencers – within reason, of course! If you'd like to talk to the coach about your child and hear about their progress or discuss any issues, it is better to email or briefly ask for an informal meeting, rather than approaching your coach and expecting an in-depth discussion before, during or after a club session, or at a competition, when coaches can often be distracted and too busy to find time to talk to you in detail. It might, of course, take a few days to find a mutually convenient time to meet, but if a coach doesn't find time to speak to fencers' parents at all over a long period of time, then you have a right to be concerned. The other side of the coin is that, whatever your concerns or questions, an experienced coach in a good club will have seen it all before, so make sure you are being rational and objective in raising a concern, and not wasting both the coach's and your valuable time!

Most fencing coaches love what they do – if you don't feel that your child's coach is passionate about their profession and the sport, and doesn't care about the progress of their athletes, then look elsewhere. But it is important to keep in mind that there are many other parents with children who share the same ambitions, hurdles and pressures (and possibly some of them *might* even be more demanding than you!), and the coach's time is finite and thinly spread. If you follow those guidelines of respecting the coach's free time and professional opinions, and communicate positively with them, they will appreciate it and will probably give you much more of their time and expertise than you might expect.

While you may only have one (or possibly two, or even three) fencing children to think about, the coach has dozens of fencers, and each one should be important to the coach and the club. However, when a coach has a fencer – or more than one – competing successfully at a high level, naturally they will get additional attention. This is the nature of competitive sport, and of life in general. Appreciate where your child figures in the club system: it's OK to be near the 'bottom of the ladder' (everyone has to start there) as long as you and the child can see that they are in an environment where serious progression is achievable with time and application, and that there isn't a glass ceiling.

While high-achieving coaches will be keen to win medals today, they should also have an eye on the next generation of potential champions, so the opportunities to improve should be there for fencers on every rung of the ladder.

When you do approach your child's coach with a question or a concern, think about how you might frame the conversation constructively. Jon, who has coached every conceivable level of fencer from 6-year-olds with foam sabres to Olympians, and has wide experience in dealing with parents of all these athletes, as well as support staff and other coaches, says:

The best way to approach your child's coach is positively and with diplomacy. Every coach will have heard complaints or criticisms, both justified and unjustified, many times before. Parents can sometimes lose perspective on their individual child's level, progress or achievements, and coaches can sometimes be sensitive to criticism of their training plans or coaching support. Fencing is a long game – it takes many years for a youngster to develop into a consistent and accomplished fencer – so remember that it's better to ask the expert their opinion first rather than try to tell them how it is. It's important to bear in mind that results are not always the only key indicator of potential in a very young fencer – although they are of course very motivating for fencer and parent alike! If you feel confident the coach has a good training plan and your child is progressing, then trust the coach to get on with their job. If, after checking on yourself, you are clear that you need to raise something with the coach, be open-minded, courteous and give them time to respond or to arrange a meeting.

Dos and don'ts

Don't say: "I was really disappointed with James's result. Why isn't he doing better? He's training hard and I'm paying for three lessons a week!"

Do say: "How do you feel James is progressing? I don't want him to get disheartened because of competition results. If he isn't on track, is there anything I can do to help him along and improve his confidence?"

Don't say: "Maria is really upset that you weren't at her piste, coaching her during the pool matches. She would have done so much better if you'd been there!"

Do say: "Maria really seems to benefit from feedback during competition, and she feels she could have done better last weekend. Is there anything we can do to help to prepare her for the occasions when a coach isn't at the side-line to support her?"

> Remember, coaches are often stretched thinly in the club and at competitions, and sometimes they have to make value judgements as to where to spend their limited time, but at the same time a good coach will help fencers and, if necessary, parents to be prepared and deal with this.

Most, though not all, clubs in the UK are run by volunteers with contracted-in coaches, or by entrepreneurial coach/managers. In the USA, many larger clubs have a professional business structure with coaches employed part-time or full-time and a manager or coach-manager, and often admin support. Club structure varies from nation to nation, and within countries too, so it's helpful for you to gain an understanding of the structure and hierarchy of your training environment. Knowing who's who and what their roles and responsibilities are will help you to understand how, and with whom, to communicate.

Daniela says:

> As a parent, I've observed coaches first-hand in three

different countries. Our family has moved around a fair amount, and so my son has moved from a French club to a Swiss club and latterly to a UK club, maintaining friendships and connections within both the French and Swiss clubs. I've seen some coaches (not at clubs we stayed at!) who wouldn't bother coming to competitions on a Sunday, and others who came but spent their whole time yelling at the kids. As a parent, here is what I look for in a fencing coach for my boys:

A good role model: someone the kids can look up to, in terms of their character, dedication to the sport and work ethic in the club.

A coach who is present: The greatest coach doesn't really help if he or she is never there at important competitions. Generally speaking, at least one coach from your club should come often to support fencers at competitions. Of course, fencers also need to learn to be self-sufficient, but the presence of a coach gives them confidence and can help in difficult situations.

Someone who knows how to motivate kids: a coach who understands their psychology, knows how to work with individuals of different strengths and different characters, and cares not only about their results but also about their personal improvement.

A coach who can find some time for your child: You mustn't have unrealistic expectations – be as dispassionate and objective as possible when you consider this and try to put yourself in the coach's shoes. But if a coach can never be bothered and *always* has other important things to do, give serious thought to looking elsewhere.

Of course, especially in the USA, high-level success in fencing is a good gateway to a college scholarship, but don't let this be all that your child's fencing is about. The life lessons and character-building inherent in the sport are more valuable than any other more tangible outcome. The college place can be one outcome of high-quality training, good coaching and successful competing, but it shouldn't be the main objective! Fencers (and sportspeople in general) who focus on the intrinsic benefits of their training and competing, rather than the potential extrinsic ones, tend to be happier and more successful!

While it is completely acceptable to ask for periodic updates, to ask questions of, or to exchange information with, your child's coach, there can be other valuable resources available too. Don't forget that other parents at the club have been through this process before, and they can be a mine of helpful information. Most parents are willing to chat and share their experiences, and in return, as you learn the ropes, you can help to pass on knowledge to newcomers to your club.

Advice about competition travel, places to stay, what equipment works (or doesn't work) for their children, and much more, can be obtained from other parents at the club. Don't be shy about asking for advice, and graciously providing it when you are asked. Although fencing is an individual sport, a fencing club is (or should be!) a community. If you show you care about others by offering advice and support, then others will hopefully reciprocate and care about your child too. You should be there as a team to cheer for all the fencers when they do well, and to support them when they don't. Competitive fencing may most often be an individual sport, but fencing training is a team sport. Fencers need one another to be able to train effectively, and while rivalry and competitiveness is healthy, it shouldn't spill over into unpleasantness. Good coaches and healthy club environments will be able to handle situations where frustration or clashes of personality cause issues, so allow them time to sort out any minor problems that may occur. But in the unlikely event that you feel that the coach is exacerbating the problem, deliberately creating conflict, or unfairly taking sides, then you need to consider whether this is the club for you.

Daniela says:

One of the most successful fencers at my son's French club was also the most generous and supportive of all the club's members. He was a confident young man who usually finished on the podium, but nevertheless found the time to encourage some of the less strong boys and offer support and advice, as did his parents. It was no wonder, therefore, that he always got a lot of support, usually when fencing in the final!

If you feel you have something positive to offer the club, you want to be more involved, and perhaps influence the club's culture in a positive way, why not consider giving some help as a volunteer? Many clubs are desperate for volunteers in areas such as fundraising groups; club armoury; committee membership; management of social media; compilation and distribution of press releases; website design and management; safeguarding and welfare, and more!

If you have expertise and/or time to offer, usually your help will be gratefully received, and volunteering can be rewarding and fun. Equally, you shouldn't be offended if your offer is turned down, as some clubs don't use volunteers in these capacities, or might already have sufficient support in these areas.

Remember:
- When raising an issue with the coach, consider objectively if your concern or question is valid, or if you're being over-protective or interfering!
- Frame your communication constructively and positively.
- Respect the coach's expertise and ask for advice rather

than complain!
- Don't be scared to ask other parents for advice, and be equally generous to newcomers with your own knowledge.
- Learn about your club's management structure and hierarchy.
- Offer to help out as a volunteer if you want to be a positive influence on the club and its culture.
- Have a rational perspective on your child's progress, performance and place in the club, but once you've checked on yourself to make sure you're doing this, trust your instincts!

Chapter 7

Winning versus improving

Relative Age Effect, playing the long game and avoiding shortcuts

As in all sports, the children who win or are successful as very young fencers are not always those who go on to success at a later stage. The 'Relative Age Effect' is a well-known phenomenon in sports where a strong physique is a big advantage, and 'Month of Birth Bias' has a particularly strong influence on the progression of athletes involved in team sports with age group cut-off dates. We will explain these effects below, as we also see them in individual skill-based sports – although the outcomes can be quite different. Although the term Relative Age Effect (RAE) is often interchangeable with the phrase Month-of-Birth Bias (MOBB), many coaches in fencing, and other sports, make a subtle differentiation between the two categories.

Let's look at RAE first, especially with reference to fencing, as RAE is somewhat more straightforward to explain: RAE simply refers to biological versus chronological age. Two fencers may be born on the same day, but one will develop biologically more quickly than the other. We've all seen the 11-year-old child who is by far the biggest and strongest in their class or club. This child is biologically older than, although chronologically a similar age to, their contemporaries. In fencing, the biologically older child will compete in the same age category as the less physically developed fencer, and they are likely therefore to have an early advantage of strength, reach and speed. Although this is usually not a long-term advantage, it can still result in mistaken 'talent-spotting', neglect of other skills development which is required in the long term, and over-praising of winning versus good quality of performance. RAE has a more fundamental effect on the long-term outcome of a participant's chances in selective team sports, such as rugby, ice hockey or football, than it does in skill-based individual sports, as in team sports the less-developed youngster may not be selected for teams and can be side-lined far more often. This leads to a deficit of game experience and loss of motivation for the individual. By contrast, athletes involved in more individual sports are usually free to enter individual events regardless of their physical development, and so they will still have opportunities to gain game experience and develop their skills.

MOBB refers to the advantage to participants in youth age-group categories who are born early in the calendar year or season cut-off date. For example, a sport with a January 1 cut-off date to determine a participant's age category will favour athletes born nearer to the cut-off date. A youngster born on January 2 can be almost a year older than a fencer born on December 31 of the same year, but they will compete in the same age category – for an U9 (Under 9) participant this is obviously more than 10 per cent of their entire lifespan! An example of this can be seen within fencing in the UK: the well-known Leon Paul Junior Series (LPJS) tournaments use January 1 as the cut-off date to determine a fencer's age group, ranging from U9 to U15 (Under

15). An early-birth-date youngster can be significantly older, more physically mature, more experienced and emotionally developed than a late-birth-date rival. This is not an intrinsic criticism of the system – the LPJS is an example of an excellent, successful introduction to competition for thousands of young fencers around the UK – but it is a word of warning to parents, coaches and fencers not to get too carried away by winning U9, U11 or U13 medals, especially if the medal-winner in question has an early birth-date or is biologically ahead of their chronological age.

It is clear that a bigger, stronger, faster child can pose enormous problems for the more skilful, tactically more astute but physically less-developed contemporary. The danger for the bigger and stronger fencer is that they can rely far too much on those physical attributes, failing to develop a wider set of skills. They may not even be well coordinated and be using real athletic ability, but simply have a longer reach, an awkward style to deal with, and be more intimidating! They may very well win medals at an early stage, and, encouraged by this success, keep executing actions and following tactics (and therefore developing deep-seated habits) which work against smaller, weaker, slower fencers, but will be completely ineffective later in their fencing life when their chronological and biological ages equalise, and fencers of a higher skill level can also match them physically. In a skill-based individual sport like fencing, early biological development, if handled badly, could therefore be argued to be a long-term disadvantage! However, this is only the case if the coach and fencer fail to develop other areas of their sport appropriately and focus only on cheap medals. Another effect of early success without having gone through the hard graft of good-quality fencing training is that the athlete may end up with a lazy mentality – they didn't need to train hard to win at first, and it can be a very difficult cultural shift later in their career, when hard training becomes necessary to maintain their success.

Equally, the fencer who has worked hard to acquire a wide range of skills, because they lacked early physical prowess, will be used to stringent training, some adversity and disappointment, and to dedicating hours to improvement, and this will stand them in good stead if they make the jump to world level.

Ultimately, of course, a biologically advanced youngster winning medals with good-quality technique and strong tactics will be motivated to continue, and to have a great chance of future success. It's not a disadvantage to win – winning is fun and motivational – but it is wise to be aware of the pitfalls, and to view great results at youth level objectively.

There is an enormous body of well-conducted research on this subject across a wide range of sports, from individual athletic sports such as swimming, complex tactical team sports such as rugby and ice hockey, through to skill-based individual sports like judo. In sports where there is a larger volume of participants, where talent-identification programs are very influential, where physical strength is an overwhelming advantage, and critically where selection for a team at an early age is key to gaining game experience, this can result in an enormously disproportionately large number of early-birth-date participants going on to become professional or compete at international level. In fencing the effect is unclear in the long term, and rudimentary research would suggest that the widely used January 1 birth date doesn't create a hugely disproportionate number of early-year-birth world-class fencers. This is likely to be because of the balancing effect of the negative aspects of early biological development in fencing (largely, the danger of ignoring wider skills development), which offset the early physical advantages and the motivational aspects of winning. A snapshot of the months of birth of all the world top 50 in each of the 6 disciplines and across Senior and U20 categories (giving a reasonable sample of 600 fencers of a very high level) shows that 67 athletes were born in July, 66 in January, 61 in April, 60 in June, 50 in September, 47 in March, 46 in both May and November, 45 in October, 41 in December, 37 in August and 34 in February. Moreover, the results are extremely inconsistent between weapons. In Women's Senior Foil 20 per cent of the world top 50 were born in January and 2 per cent in July, whereas in Men's Senior Sabre 22 per cent of the world top 50 were born in July and just 8 per cent in January! Although the sample size isn't very large, and there are many other factors to consider (for example, the number of babies born in different months in different countries), the indication is that RAE and MOBB are unlikely to be strong influences of long-term high-level success. This is of course good news for everyone: train hard and train effectively, and develop a wide range of skills, and early or late biological development will have little influence on your long-term fencing career!

The very best coaches will manage these issues astutely, challenging those young fencers who are physically more mature at an early stage to improve in other areas, and to develop in a direction which will be more effective in the long-term. It is easy for all involved (fencer, parent and coach) to be seduced by the glory of the regular podium finishes, and to assume that everything is going to plan! Of course, an early-developer shouldn't be viewed as being at a disadvantage, as long as the coach (and parents) manage their expectations, and ensure their other skills are developing in the right direction too.

Equally, the best coaches will encourage the less biologically developed fencers to continue to work on their technique, tactics, creativity and footwork, and will praise excellent performance, good use of tactical ideas and correct technique, regardless of whether these result in a medal. As the biological age of these fencers catches up with their chronological age, the complex fencing skills they have developed will be augmented by speed, strength, endurance, explosiveness and other physical skills, and the outcome will be a far more complete fencer, who has developed cunning use of tactics combined with strong technique to overcome the strategic problems facing them on the piste.

RAE, MOBB and physical development aside, it can occasionally be sensible to sacrifice winning for the development of a wider skills base anyway, as ultimately the best fencers will need to have developed this wide repertoire of actions to be successful at the highest level. The acquisition of these technical, tactical, mental and other skills is a long and complex process, requiring many hours of repetition, correction and trial-and-error over a long period of time. Imagine a fencer who learns only three actions: they will be able to acquire those three skills quickly, hone them to perfection, and choose which of the three they want to use at a given moment quickly and easily. They will be effective competitors in the short term. Now imagine a fencer who learns ten different actions: it will take far longer to perfect those ten skills, and critically it will be much more difficult initially to choose which of the large number of actions available to them is the best one to use in any given moment. As time goes by, the skills will become more natural and more finely honed, and will be quickly and effectively utilised under pressure. Eventually the fencer with ten actions will easily beat the fencer with three actions. The fencer with three actions will then need to take far more time to acquire the additional skills needed to be successful – learning in a layering system (simply trying to add further skills in a 'layering' process) is far more time-consuming in the long run, and the initial three actions will be more deep-seated than other skills acquired later. This means that these actions will still be dominant choices under pressure, resulting in a predictable and one-dimensional fencer. This is a phenomenon that has been well documented, including in a well-known study in Canada of the acquisition of skills in children playing rugby.

The rule-of-thumb often bandied about in coaching is that it takes 15 years for a fencer to become world-class. This is of course an enormously variable number, and just as with

Malcolm Gladwell's famous '10,000 hours of purposeful practice', it is an attention-grabbing headline which doesn't do justice to the complex processes of skills acquisition, personal variations in maturation, variations in training opportunities and environment, and the existence, or not, of 'talent'. It is absolutely clear, however, that thousands of hours of high-quality training over a period of years are necessary to excel in fencing, and that early results should not be at the expense of development of the overall skill-set.

Winning is great fun, but excellent performances do not always result in a medal, and other qualities should be praised and encouraged too. In younger athletes, the best coaches will value good movement, creative tactical ideas, good use of techniques, the ability to listen and adapt and a determined and focused mind over and above just winning medals. The real risk in trying to develop wider skill-sets in young fencers is that they can become disillusioned if they see others 'doing better'. It is therefore important to reinforce their achievements, perhaps occasionally put them into a weaker competition so they have their moment on the podium, and to praise good quality of performance, good tactical choices and good execution of actions, even if they don't result in a win!

In summary, as biological and chronological ages equalise over time, all fencers who train well will be able to mature into the athlete necessary to be successful. But a big, strong, fast athlete will find it extremely difficult to break early bad habits and acquire those other vital skills needed for success later in their fencing life. Be prepared to sacrifice short-term gain for excellent technique, footwork, tactics and creativity, and you will reap the rewards later!

Months of birth of the world's top 50 Seniors and Juniors (U20) in each of the six disciplines (men's and women's foil, épée and sabre) on 1 June 2018

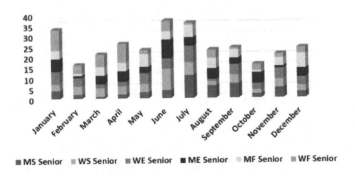

Senior Top 50 - All weapons

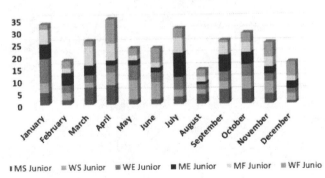

Junior Top 50 - All weapons

Junior and Senior combined. Total sample = 600

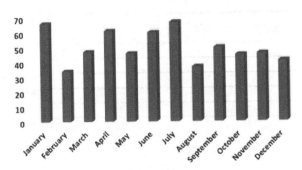

OVERALL TOTALS

Chapter 8

Athlete responsibility

The importance of self-sufficiency

From a very early age – a year old, or even younger – children are beginning to learn the skills needed to become self-reliant and resourceful later in life. Some familiar early steps towards acquiring these attributes include teaching our children to feed themselves, brush their own teeth, wash and dress themselves, and a host of other life skills. We let them get on with many of these tasks (even if they are less than competent at first), because we know they will have to learn them to survive in the real world as they get older.

The satisfaction that young children get from accomplishing what initially seems to them to be a complex task, and which requires a degree of knowledge, skill, spatial awareness and coordination, will usually result in increasing self-confidence and self-reliance further down the road. This may seem like stating the obvious, but if we look at many parents in the world of sport, it is quite surprising how deeply young sportspeople are micro-managed. Many will never learn to carry out basic tasks associated with their sport which will almost certainly stand them in good stead later, and help to boost self-reliance, resilience and resourcefulness in many areas.

Ultimately, athletes must make their own decisions on the field of play, often in a split second, which can make or break their competition, their season, and even, at the highest level of sport, their career. They need to develop the confidence to analyse and plan quickly, take calculated risks and trust their decisions. Inevitably, situations will arise when support and advice isn't available or it's impractical to offer it, and at these key moments a good competitor is able to find their own answers. While it's great to have a coach to advise, encourage and support during events, sometimes that option isn't available, and in any case the fencer must take ultimate responsibility for their performance, and not always simply rely on the knowledge and advice of others. The ability to make good decisions and follow them through is a learned skill like any other, and the athlete must be given space along the way to make their own mistakes and learn from them.

Additionally, fencers need to develop the skills required for 'smart training', to ensure they get the best from their time at training sessions, where constant support and guidance may not always be available. A fencer will need a good coach and sparring partners to reach a high level, but if they don't develop self-awareness in their fencing, and are not able to be their own best coach, they are far less likely to display some of the essential characteristics of high-performing athletes later in their career.

Developing this self-reliance and responsibility for one's performance is a gradual process, and the work starts early on by giving the fencer incrementally increasing responsibility for small things. For example, looking after their own kit and packing it before competitions, or being responsible for their water bottle and towel at competitions. It is very common (and understandable) to see a parent standing near the piste with a bottle and towel – often this is simply because the parent feels protective towards their child, and they want to be nearby at a time that can be stressful; sometimes it's so the parent feels that they have some degree of involvement and control. Rarely is it because the child is incapable of looking after a towel and a bottle of water themselves!

A good example of a step towards athlete responsibility is allowing the fencer to be responsible for their equipment. This can be a gradual process: at first you can pack the fencer's kit with them before a competition or before training. After a few weeks, you could move on to putting a checklist together with the fencer, and then they can begin to pack their own kit and tick off items as they go. At first you might want to check it afterwards to be sure (better to do this when the child isn't there!). As previously noted, a checklist will avoid the possibility of being landed with a hefty kit bill or going through the stress of trying to borrow kit if the fencer arrives at a competition having forgotten their mask or jacket!

Once a skill or a process like this has been learned, the fencer should be trusted to carry it out. Of course, they will sometimes make a mistake, forget an item or leave things to the last minute. This is part of the learning process, and ultimately taking responsibility for their own training, kit, competitions and performances will give the fencer a greater sense of control and confidence in difficult situations. In turn, this will lead to more capable and street-wise teen and adult fencers and human beings!

As parents, we very often feel responsible for our children – the way they behave, the way they organise themselves; even the way they perform on the piste. It can sometimes be hard to know when to let go, and when to allow them to take responsibility. Some aspects of this can be discussed with your child's coach, as they progress in their fencing, but sometimes it is simply a matter of common sense, and putting natural protective instincts on one side when they are clearly an overreaction to the fact that your child is nervous, or feeling pressured or desperate to perform, and you want to protect them emotionally from a possible negative outcome. In a fascinating article entitled 'Super Champions, Champions, and Almosts: Important Differences and Commonalities on the Rocky Road', Dave Collins, Aine MacNamara and Neil McCarthy analyse the results of interviews with 54 world-class athletes across a range of sports. The common denominators between 'super champions' include a love of training (not only of 'playing' or 'competing'), an obsessive perfectionism, and importantly a degree of challenge in the earlier stages of their sport. Athletes for whom all obstacles are removed at an early stage will be far less able to deal with the inevitable challenges as they move through the levels of their sport. These later career challenges could include a long trough in performance, a change of coach or training environment, missing out on selection for a major event, an injury, or any other factor that may require patience, resilience and determination.

Jon says:

> There are many ways in which parents consciously or unconsciously try to have some control or influence over their child's fencing, and usually it is with the best possible motives. Parents are emotionally (and financially) invested in their child's success, but this can lead to 'helicopter parenting', and can have a detrimental effect in the long run. Some good examples include offering fencing advice to a child when you're not a coach or experienced fencer; carrying your child's equipment, water or towel around for them at competitions; never stepping back from the side of the piste and watching from a distance or location where the child

doesn't notice you; going to every single competition with your child, even when there are opportunities for parents to share the burden of transport or for the child to travel as part of a club or squad. None of these is individually a terrible thing to do, but cumulatively over time they can lead to the fencer being reliant on others instead of on themselves. Children who have been intensely supervised in this way tend to have more anxiety about their performance and results, a less-developed ability to use initiative and take calculated risks, and poorer problem-solving skills. Allowing your child to make mistakes on and off the piste allows them to find ways to solve problems which will inevitably arise in their fencing career – and in life in general!

Daniela says:

One recent 'incident' that I personally experienced with my son's coach – Jon – was at a training camp in Italy. Many of the younger children on the camp were accompanied by parents who took the opportunity for a holiday break and some tourism. The children stayed together in one hotel with staff and coaches, and the parents made their own accommodation arrangements nearby. In my case, it was a working holiday/ writing retreat, and after a few days, I offered to take some of the boys' T-shirts to wash at the apartment where I was staying. It was extremely hot and humid, so after several days of intense training there were quite a few T-shirts in need of a wash! When I came to collect dirty washing from the fencers, I was met by a less-than-pleased Jon. "They can work out how to do their own washing, in the sink or at a launderette! It's part of their fencing equipment, and it's up to them to deal with that at a training camp," he said.

As a parent, it can be difficult to allow your child to become independent, especially when they are just getting into their teenage years. We are so used to caring for them and doing things for them, we don't realise that – especially as athletes – the self-reliance skills they develop will serve them not only later in life, but also in the short term, as they slowly become more resilient and less dependent on us.

It is important that they have the tools to manage themselves when on their own, and this includes controlling their behaviour on and off the piste, managing their kit and equipment, and yes – knowing how to wash their own T-shirts in a sink if they run out of clean clothes in a foreign country!

Parental involvement in sport has been examined closely in many studies. In the same article quoted earlier, the 'Super Champions' generally describe encouraging but not overly involved parents, whereas the 'Almost' group generally describes what are often referred to as 'pushy parents'. The level of parental involvement is broken down into 'under-involved', 'moderately involved' and 'overly involved'. Moderately involved parents are usually emotionally supportive, encourage and praise good performance, commitment and hard work as well as good results, are prepared to be involved when needed (for example, being financially supportive, giving up their time to drive to and from training, helping to arrange car-sharing for competitions) and will see the holistic benefits to the child of training and competing.

While good early results can be helpful in creating the commitment to the sport, to achieve long-term success a young fencer must work hard and be committed over a long period of time, so a love of training and competing, and a feeling of reward and well-being when pursuing their passion is an essential ingredient to long-term success. Parents who are under-involved (not supportive, don't want to enable the child to get to training or competitions, discourage the child from spending time and effort on their sport) and those who are over-involved (criticise performance, don't allow the child any independence or control of their sport, are negative towards and apply pressure to fencers, coaches and/or officials) will create an environment which leads to less enjoyment, more anxiety, and a reduced likelihood of longevity in the sport.

Results at a high level usually come from well-adjusted, resilient and complete athletes who can solve problems, deal with adversity, cope with pressure and ultimately keep their motivation to train and compete through a love of their sport.

While there may be some notable and famous exceptions to these guidelines, the statistics and the majority of profiles of world-class athletes across many sports tell us that you will give your child the best chance of success by:

- being supportive and positive
- understanding the holistic benefits of involvement in sport
- giving the fencer a degree of control over their sport: enabling but not dictating
- not carrying out tasks for the fencer, but instead doing what is necessary to facilitate them carrying out those tasks themselves
- seeing technical, physical, tactical and psychological development as being just as important as their results, especially in the younger fencer.

Chapter 9

Sports psychology 101

Attitude, resilience and dealing with pressure

© Lee Kyu Gin

Most top sportspeople and coaches, especially those involved in 'gladiatorial'-style sports, such as combat and racket sports, will tell you that the difference between the very best competitors and the 'also-rans' is largely mental or psychological. The top athletes in their fields all share a high level of technique, tactics, physical competencies and specialised fitness, so the 'mental game' is often where the margins are to be found.

But what does this really mean? How is that winning mindset developed from entering the sport to making it at the top level? And are these mental skills trainable in the same way as technical or physical skills, or are they innate in some way?

Many of the chapters in this book have already featured important aspects of psychology, in terms of attitude to training and competing, dealing with pressure, ensuring winning isn't at the expense of developing creativity, good technique or tactical awareness, being committed, and maintaining motivation. In addition, the approach and attitude of parents and coaches has a huge impact on the long-term psychological abilities of the individual fencer. While this isn't the book to give your young fencer a full psychological toolkit for their sporting life (or indeed professional or personal life), we can and should help to answer some of the questions above and begin to instil good habits which will build the foundations for long-term success. In addition, we will consider how to approach the inevitable peaks and troughs in the fencing life of a younger competitor.

Jon Rhodes is a High Performance Consultant, specialising in Sports Psychology, and has worked across a range of professional team and individual sports including soccer, tennis, rugby, judo and fencing. Jon Rhodes works closely with Jon Salfield and his athletes, aiming to develop the optimal mindset for success:

> I spend a great deal of time teaching athletes the gold nuggets of sport, only for the athlete to go home and the parent to unpick all the hard work! This is, again, where it's important for a parent to have a learning mindset over a winning mindset. I once asked a group of competitive fencers what was more important to them at this stage of their career – winning or learning? They said, learning! I then asked the same question, but this time from a different angle: 'What's more important to your parents? And what's more important to your coach?' All fencers responded with winning over learning. Additionally, a learning-focused individual will be intrinsically motivated, whereas a winning individual *may* be more extrinsically motivated.

It is important to remember that young athletes are above all children and are often going through many psychological challenges as they progress through childhood into adolescence.

Sensitive and individualised support can be a deciding factor in ensuring the progression and commitment of a young fencer. Here are some good habits and possible pitfalls you may well encounter.

1. Commitment and motivation

We have already discussed the difference between commitment and motivation, and the cumulative long-term effects of regularly missing sessions. The majority of young people give up sports participation by the age of 16–18. There are many reasons for this, not least the step change in education at that age, but one overriding factor is loss of motivation due to lack of enjoyment or disproportionate external pressure. Remember, this is your child's sport and their world. Supporting them in their passion is essential, but exerting pressure on them or being overly interfering will often result in lack of enjoyment for the fencer in training and competing, and then ultimately a greater chance of them stopping when they have the choice to do so. While you and your child may share similar goals and aspirations for their fencing, if the fencer is to succeed, ultimately the motivation and long-term commitment must come from them, not from any outside source. Allow them space to train, let them become independent over time, and let the coaches do their job!

2. Effective goal-setting

Goal-setting can be an important way of maintaining focus and motivation, giving the fencer an opportunity to review their improvement and give themselves credit for their progress, and give purpose to training and competing as the fencer develops. At the outset, the main goal is to learn about the sport and fall in love with it – this leads to dedication to training through a passion for fencing for its own sake. Quite soon, short-term goals will form naturally, such as qualifying for an age-group event, improving a technique or becoming faster. At the early stages there is no need to set formal goals, but as fencers progress this is something they should do in conjunction with their coach. Parents need not be involved, or even know and understand these goals in detail – fencers should have the right to keep them private – but ensuring that the coach and fencer have a plan to move forward is OK! Many sportspeople will have a training diary or log, but again this is a personal preference and it doesn't always work for everybody. Goals should be tangible, achievable, measurable and individualised, and they may be written or may be verbally agreed with the coach. Goals should be reviewed at intervals, and if necessary revised and clarified. The important thing is to train and compete with purpose, and strong and clear goals will facilitate this.

3. Performing well at pressure moments

Gaining experience of these pressure moments, having confidence in training, developing the tools to adapt and be creative, and gaining resilience and mental toughness will all help in the path to dealing with pressure. Learning when to take appropriate risks and having the freedom to express oneself on the piste leads to good strategic thinking and strong tactical fencing, but this must be accompanied by freedom from recrimination from coaches or parents if a good performance has culminated in defeat. Young fencers will feel nervous in competition – this is only natural, but as time goes by, and goals and expectations take shape, pressure can exert various influences. Many sportspeople use simple techniques to help them prepare for competitions: visualisation, listening to music that calms them or focuses them or fires them up before and during the event, breathing exercises and other methods of keeping the adrenalin under control. Some prefer to be left alone and retreat into their own world; others prefer to be more gregarious and burn off nervous energy by talking. For some time, a young fencer will experiment (consciously or unconsciously) with various methods of dealing with pressure.

As their experience grows, they will find their own modus operandi for competition, but if they underperform consistently when under pressure then it might be worth discussing this with the coach and considering whether some coaching in methods of dealing with pressure is required.

4. Smart training or 'deliberate practice'

Training with purpose is another subject we have discussed in previous chapters, but it is worth briefly reminding ourselves of the importance of this approach to training. It's not always good to win and bad to lose (especially in training) – sometimes developing new skills, techniques, tactics and strategies can result in a dip in performance, but fencers need to be encouraged to try out these uncomfortable and unfamiliar scenarios, and thus over time assimilate them into their game. This might mean losing more in the short term, but with the aim of being a more complete fencer with a better chance of long-term success. Fencers must be their own best coach, and make sure they're not always going through training just relying on their favourite moves – of course some sessions may be purely competitive, and then it's fine to aim only for victory, but, more often than not, there will be room for skills development during training sessions. Smart training leads to a more rounded and confident fencer, who is better able to deal with pressure.

5. Controlling the controllables

It's all too common for fencers of all ages to worry about the referee, the floor, the light in the room, the height of their opponent and other factors which are beyond their control. The most successful athletes across sports 'control the controllables' and leave the other factors to look after themselves! Making sure that the fencer is well fed, hydrated and rested, has prepared well in training, turns up early for their event, is analysing their opponents, and is trying to fence well with good tactics for the situation are all examples of controlling the controllables. A small part of this is initially your job as a parent, but most of it will be the coach's job and a learned skill on the part of your child. It's OK to discuss this attitude with your child away from the fencing environment.

In defeat, it is a common refuge to complain about the uncontrollables mentioned above. Not surprisingly, after winning, fencers will rarely complain about these factors! Making excuses for underperformance, rather than addressing core problems, is the road to long-term mediocrity.

6. Developing resilience and dealing with injuries and setbacks

This is essential to the long-term success of any sportsperson. In the early days, it is far less likely that a fencer will have serious setbacks or injuries, and hopefully by the time they're training at a level where injury or other problems may occur, the fencer is already very committed to their sport. As a parent, it's easy to either push the fencer too hard to get through an injury or a trough in performance, or say the wrong thing, though with the best intentions! When injuries occur, often the parent will panic more than the fencer. The chances are that your coach has encountered this scenario many times before and can give guidance on whether medical advice is necessary and, if so, where to find a good professional. Sometimes you as the parent can influence the next step, which is making sure that the professional's advice is followed! Some clubs will work closely with a specific physiotherapist, and be able to handle communication and rehab in-house, but if you're not lucky enough to be in that situation you may need to communicate with the coach. The coach will need to know what limitations the injury may have on performance and adapt the fencer's training accordingly. It is healthy for a fencer to keep training appropriately through injuries, perhaps turning up to the fencing session and doing rehab exercises and any light training that is permitted. This keeps the fencer engaged and motivated. Inevitably a young fencer will be upset by this kind of setback, especially if they are forced to miss competitions or a great deal of training, but it is important to note that generally the best athletes have come back stronger both physically and mentally after an injury or some other adversity.

Do say:

- "You can use this time to work on other things and learn new skills – watching and analysing other fencers, refereeing or working out tactics you would use yourself."
- "Your coach says you should go to the salle! You can still do some technical training and work on flexibility, and you can also watch and analyse other fencers and work out tactics that you would use against them." This approach makes the fencer feel they're not falling behind, and that they're still part of the training group; they'll still be frustrated but they'll be more likely to stay motivated. Also they will be able genuinely to develop their observation and analysis skills.
- "Most top athletes have an injury at some point – this is a good test of how professional you are with your rehab and training." Using an example of a top-level competitor who is already a role model is good. And treating the rehab and modified training as a test of character and commitment is a healthy approach.

Don't say:

- "Well, you can focus on your schoolwork instead; then you'll have time to train later in the year." This may be a comfort to you, the parent, but means nothing to most children. They want to train *now*, improve *now*. Time has relative meaning at different ages: 6 months to a 10-year-old is 5 per cent of their entire lifespan to date, and probably about 10 per cent of their remembered life! Imagine being told as a 40-year-old that it would take you 2 or 3 years to get back from an injury (probably an equivalent period of time in relation to your age) – it suddenly doesn't seem such a short time, does it?

- "Don't worry, Bob had the same injury and he's winning all the U15 competitions now!" Children will often feel that they are being compared to others: telling them that a rival or friend has achieved something that they are currently unable to do doesn't empower them – it inhibits and frustrates them! You need to discuss *their* way forward, not someone else's. It's a very different matter if the example used is far removed. For example, an iconic figure in sport is a role model or an idol, someone to be emulated and perhaps even exceeded, but is not a competitor to a fencer at this level.

Jon has coached young fencers who have excelled under pressure, and others of an equal (or superior) skill level who have consistently underperformed. He says:

At an early stage it is important to emphasise the importance of learning skills, competing with development in mind and growing a passion for the sport and for training. As time goes on, expectation of results (even at a very basic level) can lead to pressure, and subsequent positive and negative reactions. Treating the mental skills of competition psychology as tools, just like good fencing technique, is a healthy approach. On our high-performance program, we start off with Jon Rhodes taking group workshops discussing how people react in certain situations, and how the individual fencers feel in competition. He introduces various techniques employed by athletes to deal with these situations, and fencers are then given time to try out these techniques and come back and report on them. Fencers are free to adapt and use anything they like, and discard what doesn't work for them, like mini-researchers. Later in a fencer's career, one-to-one psychology may be a useful tool, but it shouldn't be the first port of call for a young fencer. If psychology is something that a fencer does when they've 'failed' in some way, it will simply add to the problem. Using it as another skill to be developed over time will lead to a more resilient and self-aware fencer and human being!

Just as in fencing coaching, strength and conditioning, and other learning areas, there are excellent, average and poor practitioners. As fencers begin to specialise and compete at the higher levels, they will have more individualised coaching programmes, perhaps advice and coaching for strength and conditioning, and maybe one-to-one sports psychology. It's important to make sure that any professional involved at this stage has a good reputation, a record of success, and that your fencing coach approves of this step and is to some extent involved in the work that is being done.

Although we have only looked at rudimentary examples of dealing with pressure, setbacks and other psychological issues which may be typical for a young up-and-coming fencer, this is a good starting point at the entry level. As time goes on, serious sportspeople will begin to learn mental skills, just as they learn physical ones, and – as with physical skills – some will find certain aspects of this more difficult than others. There are many excellent publications on sports psychology and performance psychology, but in the early years the most important foundations for psychological well-being and success are, as we know by now, smart training, freedom to fence without pressure from parents, confidence in training, a range of skills and a passion for and love of the sport.

Further reading

Duckworth, A. (2016). *Grit: The power of passion and perseverance.* New York: Scribner.

Dweck, C. (2017). *Mindset – updated edition: Changing the way you think to fulfil your potential.* London: Hachette.

Kahneman, D., and Egan, P. (2011). *Thinking, Fast and Slow.* New York: Farrar, Straus and Giroux.

Syed, M. (2010). *Bounce: How champions are made.* London: HarperCollins.

Daniela says:

As my son started competing in France at the age of 9, he was used to big events, with at least 50 fencers and often up to 150, or more. That made him less nervous in bigger competitions, because he was quite used to the large number of potential opponents, to the noise and the size of the venue. I noticed that some of the fencers who were less used to large events were more nervous at first, but most of them quickly got used to the change from 'small competitions' to 'bigger ones'.

However, when Roman's French friends started competing internationally, they were in for quite a shock at first: they were indeed used to big events with lots of fencers and noise, but they were not used to opponents with different styles of fencing, and to different styles of refereeing. All these took a while to get used to, but in the end, if your child is hoping to compete internationally, they (and you!) ultimately will have to get used to both the size of the competitions and the different styles of fencing and refereeing. It might take a few competitions to get to that point, so certainly don't expect excellent results at first. Your fencer will usually need some time to make that switch – which is mostly mental, as their style of fencing and technical ability goes with them wherever they compete!

Once the fencer has the competition bug and has decided they want to do more, it is a good idea to build up their confidence by helping them get used to larger events with more competitors gradually, without it being a shock to them. Moving too quickly to larger competitions might hinder their performance and their confidence in the future, as they might, of course, not do well straight away. Once again, your coach will be able to advise on the progression through different levels of competition. Climbing rankings, whether U9 local rankings or national U17 rankings, should not be a primary consideration – quality of performance, progression and commitment should come first.

As a parent, it can be overwhelming to accompany your pre-teen to a large professional-seeming venue, when perhaps until now they have only fenced a handful of opponents in a local gym converted to a fencing salle.

One simple step to calming the pre-event nerves can be to visit the venue before the start of the competition – of course you may not always be able to arrive well in advance the previous evening, but if you do it's a good idea to 'recce' the venue. You might want to check the location so you can find it easily, whether it's straightforward to park there, and whether there are shops around in case you need to stock up on anything (although it's a good plan to bring the fencer's supplies whenever possible). Many stressed parents (and as a result, even more nervous children!) arrive at competition venues at the last minute because they got lost or couldn't find parking!

If the venue is open (perhaps there is another competition going on, for a different age-group or category, or the organising team might be setting up equipment) you can have a quick peek inside: are there different fencing halls? Where are the changing rooms and toilets?

Arriving on time at a venue that isn't totally unfamiliar is far less stressful and allows the fencer to 'control the controllables' far better. Obviously, over time you might get to know the different competition venues and will know if it's a good idea to bring a packed lunch and where you can warm up in a dedicated area. But unless you know all the venues and are sure nothing has changed since you were there last, arriving early and checking all this out is a good idea.

Jon says:

As young fencers move through age groups and levels

of competitions, they face more mature and experienced opponents, and the first few times they compete after moving up a level they might of course not perform as well. Fencers may also experience renewed feelings of nervousness and stress. Essentially you are repeating the process of starting out in competition – the same messages should be reiterated: recognise that everyone is nervous; recognise that your brain can push you into poor decision-making when you're nervous and that the answer is to fall back on the good fencing actions and tactics used in training; emphasise improvement and learning as fencers move to a new level; praise good attitude, commitment, effort, and good fencing actions, as well as good results. In a short time, the fencer will adapt to the new level, and feel more comfortable again – until it's time for the next rung on the ladder!

Once your child is doing well at local and regional competitions, national events will start to be an option. Some clubs will have organised trips to these events, and you may not even need to attend – it's a good idea to start to loosen the apron strings and allow your child the chance to travel with their squad if this is an option.

Daniela says:

> As a parent, I know that it is not easy to let your child travel and compete alone. However, there is much to be gained from giving them this independence at an early age. Roman started boarding at Truro School at the age of 12, which I thought was a bit young – but he seemed to enjoy it despite the challenges until we moved to Truro a year later. Then we had to travel again and he again became a boarder at the age of 15 – because he wanted to be able to train at the Truro Fencing Club every day. The independence and inner

strength he gained from this experience are invaluable.

Your fencer – and you – will certainly have to make some tough decisions along the way, and it is up to every child and family to decide just how much they are willing to do for their sport. But the very minimum is indeed giving your child the experience of travelling with their squad or club and competing without you at the piste side!

Even for very young age-groups, most countries have national ranking competitions, and some have official or unofficial selection for younger fencers to compete at international competitions. These national and international events can be very motivational for a young athlete, but selection for them is not necessarily an essential part of early development.

Of course, your fencer is very likely not to qualify straight away for their dream competition and not to land at the top of the ranking at their first attempt. Your job, as a parent, is to enable them to develop the perseverance needed (not just in fencing, but in life!) to continue to compete, train, learn and then, as a result of this process, climb the rankings.

Some young people will get very frustrated if they don't do well straight away, and it may even lead them to say they want to give up competing. Not every child is going to be an international fencer – that is both inevitable and absolutely fine – but every child should be able to get intrinsic rewards from their sport. Be sure that the motivation to compete and climb the ladder comes from your child, not from you. If it does, and you and they are willing to put in the time, effort, dedication and determination, they will of course stand a much greater chance of reaching their goals.

It is useful and sensible to learn a little about your national fencing federation, how it's structured, how fencers are selected for national squads and teams, and whether they have specific programs or requirements for young fencers. Most fencing federations have selection systems based on rankings alone for younger age-groups, with elements of discretion for the make-up of teams for team events. As fencers progress through age groups, selection may become more complex. Much of this information is likely to be available on your fencing federation's website (although some trawling may be needed!), and of course your coach is likely to have a good understanding of the system.

Inevitably, as in all sports, there may be an element of politics, but almost always selections are made based on a rationale, rather than the bias that can be perceived by fencers, parents and coaches. Whether or not you agree with the rationale is, of course, another question! The key is not to get too involved in or hung up on sports politics – the reality is that any federation or group of selectors will want to pick an individual who has a huge positive impact on a team, so it is far better to aim to be that outstanding individual than it is to be outraged at seeming unfairness! Of course, if a fencer's sole aim in life is to make the U17 World Championships, and they are not selected, then they will be angry, upset and demotivated and may feel a loss of self-esteem. If this goal sits alongside other longer-term goals (achieving excellence in a certain area, becoming part of a senior team, and so on), then disappointments of this kind are likely to be channelled into renewed effort and a refocus on goals, and they can have a positive effect. Resilience and grit are key characteristics in any high-level sportsperson, and there is often more value in setbacks and challenges than in successes and a smooth path.

Chapter 11

International competitions

What to expect when you fence abroad

As your child progresses in the sport, there's a chance they may have the opportunity to fence internationally. Some clubs and coaches organise trips to international age-group events at quite an early stage, while others will wait until fencers qualify for selection events for their country at U15, U17 or U20 level. Because the US fencing circuit is so large and well populated, geographically huge, and the tournaments are generally large and fiercely competitive, it is less common for American youngsters to compete abroad regularly early on in their fencing career than for those based in many parts of Europe or Asia. Similarly, in France the domestic circuit is so large that young fencers compete abroad less often.

However, if your child reaches the level where Cadet (U17) and Junior (U20) World and Zonal Championships are on the radar, then international travel becomes an almost inevitable part of gaining top-level experience and qualifying for selection for these events.

International events can of course add a whole new layer of excitement, competition and pressure, as well as the opportunity for growth and education of the fencer. In addition to the lessons learnt directly in fencing, some of the many positive outcomes for fencers who compete internationally will be making friends around the world, being resourceful and finding ways to make themselves understood (especially where obtaining food and drink is required!), being able to negotiate transport systems in many countries, and generally having a positive and open-minded view of the wider world.

Young fencers face many challenges and learning areas at such events. These include adjusting to different time zones, eating unfamiliar food, being part of a huge event with a lot of noise and distraction, competing with very different styles of fencers, keeping focus on one's fencing performance in a strange environment, learning to deal with the pressure of international competition, adapting to different styles of refereeing and understanding the referees, fencing a whole new set of opponents, and of course the pride and excitement of being an 'international'. A number of key European youth events are very multinational, with athletes from around Europe, the USA, and sometimes Asia and North Africa. The atmosphere can be quite intense, with hundreds of fencers, coaches and supporters making a lot of noise and taking the competition very seriously. Entries can run into the hundreds, and aside from the fencing itself, the competition can be a gruelling physical and mental test! For the uninitiated, simply knowing what piste you are fencing on, and at what time, is a challenge in itself. Competitions are run in many countries and in varying age groups, often from U10 up to U15. These younger age categories are usually open events, without restriction on entry, and are not official 'internationals', but more of a training ground for youngsters to learn the skills of competing successfully. They provide an excellent stepping-stone between domestic competition and the more serious international Cadet and Junior tournaments.

If you are at a club with an experienced coach, they will be able to support you and your child in this new world, and don't be shy of speaking to parents of older fencers about their previous experiences. They may even have been to exactly the same event in the same venue in the past and can offer tips for places to eat and stay, information on the venue and other hard-earned local knowledge! If not, it's worth doing a little research online before you set off for unfamiliar territory.

Some simple things you can do which can prepare you and the fencer include:

- Packing some energy bars, snack bars and fruit that your child is familiar with and that you know they will use.
- Stocking up on some electrolyte powder or tablets, as some venues can be very hot and air conditioning is definitely not guaranteed. This means the fencer may dehydrate faster than usual, and water alone doesn't replace all the electrolytes lost through heavy sweating.
- Making sure you have some local currency, as you can't guarantee you'll find an ATM when you need one!
- Double- and triple-check fencing kit before you leave and have basic tools for changing blades or fixing wires (your coach can advise on this). If kit breaks you can't be certain there'll be an equipment trade stand.
- The coach will probably talk to the fencers about what to expect if it's their first time at such an event, but if they haven't then it's fine to ask them to have a short chat with your child to give them an idea of what the event is like.
- Sourcing bottled water before the day of competition: you might expect that every venue would have a food and drink stand or a café, but don't count on it.

- Get your child to pack a toilet roll in their fencing bag...it is not uncommon for venues in some parts of the world to run out of paper quite quickly and not bother replacing it!

As fencers grow up and 'age out' of younger age groups, they will then reach Cadet (U17) and Junior (U20) levels. These are the more official international age groups, and there are Cadet and Junior representative events for which national federations will select and enter squads. The selection system varies from country to country but is usually based on the national ranking of a fencer. Ranking points are generally scored at domestic competitions in the relevant age groups. Some countries treat the Cadet circuit less 'officially', but nevertheless they are a qualifying arena for youth major championships, and a step up from domestic or U15 events.

Here is an example of a selection system in the UK for the Cadet European Circuit:

The top 15 boys and top 15 girls in their respective national ranking are selected for the GB Cadet squad to compete on the European Circuit at events nominated by the National Governing Body for fencing in the UK, British Fencing. The national ranking is determined by a ranking points system, with points scored at the British U17 Championships, and five domestic ranking competitions in the U17 and U20 category. Selections are made for four European events at different points in the season, which runs from September to April. At the end of the season, the top three in the ranking are then selected as the GB team for the World Championships, based on their results at the European Circuit competitions. Sometimes a minimum qualifying standard is set by a Federation (for example, a fencer must make a top 32 or better, or score a certain number of points to be eligible for selection), and if too few fencers meet the qualifying standard the Federation may decide either to select on discretion or to send fewer fencers. There are U17 and U20

World Youth Championships and Zonal Championships (the four zones are Europe, Americas, Asia and Africa) in all three disciplines of foil, épée and sabre for boys and girls.

The biggest step up from youth events in terms of presentation and atmosphere is the U20 World Cup circuit. There are around eight U20 World Cups throughout the season, and these are held all around the globe, with the biggest and most multinational events taking place in Europe. The Junior World Cup events are affiliated to the international governing body for fencing, the FIE. Each nation has a limit on the number of athletes they can enter, and refereeing is by FIE-qualified world-level referees. The events become more formal and are the stepping-stone between youth fencing and Senior World Cup fencing. The level is generally very high, with the very best U20 fencers typically being part of their Senior national squad and having a great deal of competition experience, a high level of athletic and technical/tactical ability and some experience at Senior World Cup competitions.

The ultimate aim of early participation in international youth events must be to develop a wide base of experience in dealing with different opponents, environments and situations. It is very helpful for the long-term prospects of a young fencer in dealing effectively with 'crunch' moments and can also provide benchmarks for young fencers to aspire to. International success at a young age can be inspiring and motivational for fencers, parents and coaches alike, but isn't necessarily an indicator of Senior-level success.

Indeed, a large study of combat sports in Germany by Arne Gullich found that winning at U18 level was actually a negative indicator of Senior-level success! While this doesn't mean it's bad to win at an early age, the more important indicators are the fencer's commitment to training, their athletic, technical and tactical development, and their resilience and motivation in the face of adversity. These, combined with an ever-increasing bedrock of appropriate competition experience, are the foundations for a successful future.

In fencing, correlations do seem to exist between success at U20 World Cup level and longer-term success. The majority of the world's top Seniors scored a top 8 finish in a Junior World Cup and/or a Junior Championship, but there is a significant minority that didn't achieve this standard, and one should be cautious about confusing correlation and causation.

If your child gets the chance to experience international competition at an appropriate time, try to seize the opportunity and support them in gaining this experience.

Daniela says:

When my son fenced on the French circuit, up to the age of 15, it was rare for young French fencers to compete outside France. In fact, some of the fencers at my son's club have never been on an aeroplane and fencing internationally was rarely an option considered by fencing families. As already mentioned, the French circuit is very large, so local, regional and national competitions provided opportunities to fence different opponents. However, the general 'style' of fencing was similar at all the competitions on the French circuit.

The general state of mind was that if fencers qualify for the French squad then great (as the French Fencing Federation would pay for their trips abroad anyway) and if not – too bad.

When we moved to the UK and my son started fencing on the British circuit and at Truro Fencing Club, I was surprised by the dedication some families demonstrated towards fencing and towards gaining competition experience – and the resources they put into it. Even families who could not easily afford international travel prioritised fencing travel over other things such as holidays and other luxuries.

From the age of 12 (and in some cases even younger), kids

travelled with their parents and club coaches to international youth competitions in Poland, Greece, Romania and beyond. A whole new world opened up to us – as well as the understanding that international experience can indeed help young athletes prosper in many ways.

In our case, my son rarely travelled to international competitions before the age of 15, for financial reasons and the needs of our other children, but when he did, he found the experience beneficial and inspiring. As he continued fencing on both the French and British circuits and gaining more competition experience, we came to realise that fencing competitions can sometimes become 'mini holidays' with an extra day (or more, when possible) added for fun, exploration, education and tourism. This allowed us to dedicate more resources to fencing-related travel – which in turn, and on top of the commitment to training and the excellent coaching, led to great improvements in my son's results.

When I've mentioned to other (non-fencing) parents that my son competed at 'international youth events' many expressed astonishment at our dedication to the sport. My answer to this is: I believe that a huge amount of the success of young athletes is due to the commitment of their parents. Dedication of time, energy and money allows young athletes to progress, train and compete, and sets the foundations for the future. Is it a sacrifice? Possibly, but it never felt that way to me, as the benefits my son reaped, and continues to reap, from this dedication to the sport of fencing are immense and are certainly not limited to his results at local, regional, national and international competitions.

These include improved focus and concentration, perseverance, willingness to demonstrate effort and dedication to seeing things through, sportsmanship, working as part of a team, prioritising and organising commitments and even, more recently, knowing how to do his own laundry when travelling! These are life skills that he gained through the dedication to his sport, and even if he stopped fencing tomorrow, they will serve him throughout his life.

Were those early international fencing competitions worth investing in? In our case, my answer would be: "Absolutely."

Chapter 12

Fit to fence

Physiology, strength and conditioning, and nutrition

Our final chapter will look at the physiology of fencers, how sports sciences apply to fencing, and how this affects your child.

As in all Olympic sports in the modern era, fencing programs at the highest level employ up-to-date sports science to try to make the small percentage gains needed to stay ahead of the opposition. These include, but are not limited to, strength and conditioning coaches, sleep and nutrition consultants, video analysts, psychologists, physiotherapists, movement specialists, and other experts in various fields.

As a young fencer starting out in the sport, your child doesn't need specialist support, and probably won't for some time. A basic understanding of athletic development and the importance of good nutrition and sleep is all you need to start off on the right foot. We will look at some good basic principles which will help your child, not just in fencing, but in day-to-day life, especially as they get older.

First, it is important to say that fencing as a sport is something of an outlier in terms of the range of physiological types who are successful at world level. While it is true to say that generally fencers have become taller, and possibly faster, over time (due to selective programs, earlier specialisation, more scientific training methods and a more global professional environment), no single body type can be seen to be dominant. One of the wonderful aspects of fencing is that an athlete can overcome physical disadvantage (for example, a shorter reach), with excellent footwork or top-class technique and tactics. There are many sports where certain physiological requirements are essential for top-level success, and so if you lack these physiological attributes, you will simply never be able to succeed at the highest level.

Most of the physical skills in fencing are ones which can be developed from a young age, such as coordination, spatial awareness, balance and flexibility. Other attributes develop at various stages (for example, speed, power and explosiveness), and can be enhanced by good training in specific biological 'trainability' windows, and over time will be improved as a young fencer grows into a Junior and Senior international.

The key for the new fencer is to develop all-round athletic ability. A good club and coach will help very young fencers develop these skills with games and appropriate fencing-related activities. Agility and coordination games, flexibility and balance exercises, and fencing itself, will all help the development of the young fencer into a competent athlete.

As fencing is a 'one-sided' sport (that is, a right-handed fencer only uses their right arm and leads with their right leg), it is important that younger fencers remain physically active outside fencing training. Recreational participation in another sport is a great way to help general physical skills, but it will also offset the muscular imbalances which will occur from regular and intense fencing training. To clarify this, most serious fencers will have larger quadriceps, hamstring and gluteus on their dominant side (right side for a right-hander, left side for a left-hander), and a larger calf muscle on the non-dominant side. This is nothing to worry about, and actually is an adaptation of the muscles for the tasks they are being asked to carry out. This is much like left-handed people generally (and harmlessly) having a slightly stronger left than right arm. However, if these imbalances become extreme, they can lead to injury, and lack of engagement of useful secondary muscle groups.

A general guideline is that any imbalance between left and right side should be contained within a 15% margin.

Although there is not a great deal of research on this in fencing, the article 'Isokinetic strength training program for muscular imbalances in professional soccer players' (A. Gioftsidou, I. Ispirlidis, G. Pafis, P. Malliou, C. Bikos, G. Godolias, *Sport Sciences for Health*, March 2008) states that: "many researchers have supported that bilateral differences (> 15%) in muscular performance (quadriceps and hamstring) detected with isokinetic measures are important predictors of soccer players' injuries and signs of previous injuries and an incomplete rehabilitation program."

As time goes on, serious competitive fencers will generally start to follow a more specialist and personalised strength and conditioning program aimed at developing endurance, explosive power, balance, core strength and other physical attributes. A good program will also help prevent injury from hard training and competing, building in physical resilience, which, in turn, supports mental well-being and self-confidence. It is important to note that as fencers and fencing become more specialised, the physical fitness requirements of foil, épée and sabre are not at all the same. Here is a brief overview of the different requirements of the three weapons:

Foil – matches tend to last for longer periods of time, with off-target lights as well as scoring lights creating a natural stop/start characteristic. However, lengthy periods of medium-intensity movement punctuated with explosive actions also occur, and so foil requires a more all-round fitness.

Épée – a great deal of patience and discipline is required in épée, and so it leans more towards endurance fitness. Timing is more important than sheer speed, although the final action can still be explosive. Lengthy periods of medium-intensity movement with a great deal of change of distance and direction are characteristic of an épée match.

Sabre – matches are much faster, and actions are extremely explosive. Sabre requires the ability to perform anaerobic actions repeatedly with very short breaks. Intensity is high but in short bursts, and speed is combined with the ability to stop dead and change direction under control.

All three weapons require excellent flexibility, core strength, balance and coordination – so clearly a fitness/strength and conditioning coach with a good knowledge of the sport is a very useful asset!

Steve Petrie is a former MMA fighter, and now a Strength and Conditioning Coach who has designed programs for British Fencing's Development Program and leads S&C for Jon's club in Truro. Steve says:

Strength and conditioning is an important element in any athlete's journey and should run in coordination with the aims of the fencing program. Strength and conditioning coaches will work closely with the fencing coaches in supporting the development of the athletes.

A good strength and conditioning program should change and adapt to the needs of the athlete as they progress through their career. Early in the athlete's career a broad base of skills is developed – coordination, balance, core strength, speed and endurance may be worked on through games, body weight circuits and specific drills designed to achieve the desired outcome. The aim at this point is to create the neural pathways that athletes will rely on later in their careers as well as reducing the risks of injury.

A strength and conditioning coach will tailor the athlete's program as they go through puberty to reflect the way that the athlete's body is changing and the demands being placed on it, such as reduced flexibility and coordination. At this point in an athlete's career it is still important that they have exposure to a variety of different sports as this will help with qualities such as spatial awareness and decision-making.

Post puberty, athletes generally begin to specialise in a specific sport, in this case fencing. At this stage, the strength and conditioning program becomes sport specific. For example, due to the demands of the sport, a sabre program will have a greater emphasis on power training and plyometrics. It is at this point that athletes may be moving from Cadet to Junior and maybe even Senior fencing competition. In order to best prepare the athletes for competition, a periodised training program will be introduced.

Periodisation is a way of organising training into specific training blocks in order to achieve peak condition for periods of competition. This will take the form of an annual overview based on the competition calendar and will be broken down into a number of trainability windows. Athletes competing at international Cadet level through to Olympic level should have their training structured through a periodised program.

Finally it is important to remember that strength and

conditioning is to aid the development of the fencer and should complement the aims of the athlete, and their coach and program.

It goes without saying that a good balanced diet is very important, both for the general well-being of the fencer and for their ability to train and recover effectively. Day-to-day and in-competition nutrition and hydration are important factors in high-performance fencing, as in any other sport, and the basic principles of good nutrition apply:

- A balanced diet of complex carbohydrates, good-quality proteins and moderate fats
- Plenty of fresh fruit and vegetables
- Avoid simple and white carbs (refined sugars, white bread, pasta and rice) and switch to wholemeal versions
- Avoid highly processed foods, which often contain hidden fats and sugars and lack nutritional value
- Eat little and often, and take on board high-GI snacks after training for recovery
- Hydrate well, even outside training and competition

Hydration

Getting into the habit of hydrating well is very important, but young fencers can find this difficult! Poor hydration has a huge impact on the ability to perform physically, and also has significant effect on brain function.

Drinking only water during exercise isn't effective hydration, as the body sweats out not only water but also essential electrolytes (such as sodium, potassium and calcium). Heavy loss of electrolytes can lead to cramping and difficulty in absorbing fluids to rehydrate. Electrolytes are naturally replaced by good nutrition, but during heavy exercise this isn't very practical, so a good sports drink is an excellent solution. Many sports drinks contain huge amounts of sugar, and excessive consumption can lead to detrimental effects on gum health. It's easy to make a healthier alternative to sports drinks by mixing 50 per cent water and fresh fruit juice with a small pinch of salt. Alternatively, healthier sports drink options are widely available.

Over time, the young fencer will find what works for them, but if their energy is consistently low, or recovery from training or competitions is slow, then it is worth taking a closer look at overall lifestyle, nutrition and hydration.

Remember:

Good nutrition provides fuel for better performance, nutrients to help recovery and fluids to hydrate your body. A serious fencer needs to fuel training sessions, aid the body's recovery, prepare for competitions and compete effectively.

Day to day

A sensible balanced diet will help you train, perform and recover more effectively:

- Fruit and veg – eat lots. The UK recommendation is 5 portions a day for the general population. Twice that is recommended for serious athletes!
- Carbs – at breakfast and immediately before/after training. The harder you train, the more carbs you need.
- Dairy – provides vital minerals but should be eaten in moderation as it is often high in saturated fat. Be cautious of low-fat options, as they often contain increased levels of sugar.
- Protein – vital for repair and recovery from training and competition. Lean protein sources are best: white meat, fish, beans, pulses, and so on.
- Fats – junk food, animal fats and processed fats are high in saturates and should be minimised. Olive oil, eggs,

nuts and seeds provide useful unsaturated fats and can be eaten regularly in moderation.

- Hydrate! Drink regularly throughout the day.

Training

2–3 hours before training:

- Hydrate well – use isotonic drinks, which contain higher levels of carbs, as well as electrolytes which aid the absorption of water.
- Eat a light meal rich in complex carbohydrates and protein, and low in fat (for example: baked potato and beans, rice with chicken, wholemeal pasta with a light sauce).
- Can't eat before competing/training? Try using a high carb/protein sports drink, low fat milkshake or smoothie.

During training:

- Hydrate well during training. Hypotonic drinks (low in carbs) are ideal for rapid rehydration in short training sessions (2 hours or less).

After training:

- The body recovers from exercise more quickly if it is immediately fuelled with a high-GI drink or snack. Try a cereal bar, jaffa cakes or recovery shake. Depleted glycogen in the muscles is restored more effectively if this is done within the 'golden hour' of finishing training.

Competition

The day before competition:

- Eat small amounts of protein and carb-rich foods every

2–3 hours.
- Hydrate as much as you can – isotonic drinks and water.

The day of competition:

- Breakfast should be light and be a combination of simple and complex carbs, and protein. Hydrate well.
- Hydrate throughout the day. Drink hypotonic drinks during short breaks, and use isotonic drinks when you have a longer break.
- Thirst is not a good indicator of dehydration – if you are thirsty then you are already dehydrated. Drink little and often *before* you feel thirsty.
- Snack throughout the day on lower-fat, higher-carb snacks.
- Sometimes sportspeople find it difficult to eat on the morning of competition – a combination of nerves and adrenalin can create a nauseous feeling, or simply leave the fencer feeling unable to eat. A good solution to this would be to try a homemade smoothie – there are many online resources for good, balanced smoothie recipes which can help replace a solid breakfast. A good-quality protein shake or low-fat milkshake (perhaps with some oats and peanut butter added!) is also a helpful alternative.

Immediately after competing:

- Help your body to recover with a high-GI drink or snack.
- 1–3 hours after competing, refuel with a high-carb low-fat meal.

Jon says:

Don't become obsessed with S&C (strength and conditioning)

and nutrition at an early stage – focus on common sense, a good balanced diet, good hydration and general good fitness. Ultimately, fencing skills are the primary requirement for a good fencer – the best S&C and sports science program in the world will not be helpful if either the fencer doesn't engage with it, or if it has a detrimental effect on their ability to carry out the right level of fencing skills training. Any work done outside the fencing salle which is aimed at improving fencing performance should be cleared with your fencing coach first. At a later stage, an experienced and knowledgeable S&C coach, and a professional approach to lifestyle, diet and hydration can help make small percentage gains; but for now, focus on supporting the young fencer in learning, falling in love with and committing to this amazing sport.

Conclusion

We have looked in some detail at many aspects of the sport of fencing, and how best to operate within the fencing environment as a fencer and as a fencing parent. Our discussion has ranged across the basic rules of the sport and some of its history, a look at equipment, training, skills development, communication, competing, and of course some key points on the psychology and mindset which will help long-term success, and some aspects of fitness training and nutrition.

Good training, appropriate competition and the right mindset will build confidence, self-reliance, resourcefulness, resilience and creativity, as well as a network of new friends, and a fitter and stronger mind and body. These will all add to the likelihood of achieving goals like international representation or a sports scholarship. But if, at the early stages, these are the only focus of the fencer, over and above developing a passion for the sport and committing to training, then those goals are far less likely to be achieved. Allow your child to inhabit their own world of fencing, and support them along the way, and you will maximise their chances of success, while enhancing their development as a person.

A final word from Jon:

Fencing is a wonderful sport which can transform young people with its extraordinary challenges and the range of skills it demands. At the highest level it is one of the most complex, absorbing and exciting sports in which to compete.

If you encourage and support your child to pursue their goals in fencing, and allow them to own their sport, you will see positive outcomes for them far beyond simply being a successful competitor. Good luck!

And from Daniela:

Being a parent of a motivated fencer carries challenges beyond all the other usual challenges of parenting. The commitment can of course be immense – but it is important to note that most, if not all, successful athletes have a large degree of parental support. It is much more likely that your child will 'make it' as an athlete if they know they have support from their family, but this should not be confused with pushing them to compete and to achieve – the motivation has to come from them. We are just their support-crew, and we hope that this book will help many parents of motivated fencers learn more about how to become the best support-crew possible!

Glossary of fencing terms

A

Absence of blade When the blades of the two fencers are not touching; the opposite of engagement.

Advance A fencing step forward.

Advance-lunge An advance followed immediately by a lunge.

Allez (French for 'go'). The word used by the referee to start or restart a match.

Assault A friendly combat between two fencers, where score may or may not be kept, and is not a part of any competition.

Attack The initial offensive action.

Attaque au fer An attack against the opponent's blade.

Avertissement (Also **yellow card** or 'warning') A warning card issued for a minor rule infraction by one of the fencers. A second yellow card offence by a fencer is punished by a red card, and thus the awarding of a point to the opponent.

B

Balestra A short jump forwards, immediately followed by a lunge, though it is common in many countries for 'balestra' to refer to only the jump.

Beat A sharp controlled blow to the middle or top third of the opponent's blade, with the objective of provoking a reaction or creating an opening.

Black card The black card is used to sanction the most serious disciplinary offences in a fencing competition. The offending fencer is expelled immediately from the event or tournament, regardless of whether he or she had any prior warnings. A black card can also be used to expel a third party disrupting the match. Subsequent longer-term bans may be enforced.

Body wire or cord An insulated wire that runs under a fencer's jacket, connecting the weapon to the scoring equipment. The body wire also connects to the electric jacket or **lamé**.

Bout (USA) *or* Match (UK)

An assault at which score is kept. Usually refers to a match between two fencers in a competition.

C

Cadet The Under 17 age-group category, and the youngest category at which World and Zonal Championships are held every year.

Circular parry A parry that moves in a circle, collecting the opponent's attacking blade on the way, and ending up in the same position in which it started.

Compound attack An attack or riposte incorporating one or more actions. A compound attack may incorporate disengages, beats, and so on, as long as it is a continuous attack.

Compound riposte A riposte made with one or more actions. A riposte may incorporate disengages, beats, and so on, as long as it is continuous.

Corps-à-corps (French for 'body-to-body') The action of two fencers coming into physical contact with one another with any portion of their bodies. In foil and sabre this is against the rules and will cause the referee to halt the fencing action. In épée, it is not against the rules, but contact may not be accompanied with any brutality or force (intentional or not).

Counter-attack An attack made against, or into, an attack initiated by the opponent. In foil and sabre, a counter-attack does not have the right of way against the opponent's attack. Counter-attacking is a common tactic in épée, which doesn't have right-of-way rules, so one can make a touch by hitting first.

Counter-beat (Also 'change-beat') A beat that is preceded by a circle under the opponent's blade.

Counter-riposte A second, third, or further riposte in a fencing 'phrase' or encounter. A counter-riposte is the offensive action following the parry of any riposte. They are numbered so that the riposte is the offensive action following the successful parry; the first counter-riposte is the offensive action following the parry of the riposte, the second counter-riposte follows the parry of the first counter-riposte, and so on.

Counter-time An action that responds to the opponent's counter-attack, usually a parry of the counter-attack followed by a riposte.

Cross-over An advance or retreat made by crossing one leg in front of the other. In sabre,

crossing the feet while moving forwards
is prohibited.

Cut   An attack made with the edge of the
blade. Cuts are only valid in sabre.

D

Derobement   Avoidance of the opponent's attempt to
entrap, beat, press or take the blade.

Direct   An attack or riposte that finishes in the
same line in which it was formed, with no
feints.

Disengage   A movement of the blade underneath and
around the opponent's blade, finishing
on the opposite side of the blade.

Displacement   Moving the target to avoid an attack;
dodging.

Double   A double touch. In épée, two attacks
that arrive within 40 milliseconds of
each other, resulting in a touch for both
opponents. In foil and sabre, double
touches use right-of-way to determine
who is awarded the point.

Dry (USA) *or* Steam (UK)

Fencing without electric scoring
equipment.

E

En garde   (French for 'on guard') Spoken at
the beginning of a bout to bring the
participants into the starting position.

Engagement   During an encounter between two
fencers, the point at which the fencers are
close enough to join blades, or to make
an effective attack. Blade contact is also

referred to as an engagement.

Épée
A fencing weapon with a V-shaped cross-section blade and a large round guard.

Extension
The simplest attacking action. An offensive action consisting of extending the sword arm forwards.

F

Feint
An offensive movement initially resembling an attack with the intention of changing to another line before the attack is completed. A feint is intended to draw a reaction from an opponent.

Flèche
(French for 'arrow') The rear leg is thrown in front of the front leg and the fencer sprints past their opponent. This action is not allowed during sabre bouts, because the front and rear legs must not cross.

Flick
A whipping movement of the foible of the blade to strike at a concealed target. Used in foil and épée.

Flunge
A portmanteau of 'flèche' and 'lunge' – the sabre version of a 'flèche'. The fencer executes a forward jump in the air, but unlike in the flèche, the rear leg is not brought in front of the front leg to ensure compliance with the rules.

Foible
The top third of the blade. This section of the blade is weaker, and is used for beats and other actions where speed is more important than leverage.

Foil
A fencing weapon with a rectangular cross-section blade and a small round guard, descended from the practice

	weapon of the eighteenth century for small-sword fighting.
Forte	The bottom third of the blade, so named as it is the strongest part of the blade (French *fort(e)* = strong). Ideally the forte is the part of the blade used to perform a parry.
Forward recovery	A recovery from a lunge, performed by pulling the rear leg up into en garde, rather than pulling the front leg backwards.
French grip	A traditional handle with a long, slightly curved grip and a large pommel.

G

Guard	(Also 'bell' and 'bell guard') A cup-shaped metal weapon part which protects the hand. Foils use small concentrically mounted guards, épées use larger offset-mounted guards, and sabres have a distinctive knuckle guard that wraps around the handle to protect the hand from cuts.

H

Hilt	The main parts of the sword apart from the blade, consisting of guard, grip, and pommel.

I

Indirect	An attack or riposte that finishes in a line different from that in which it was formed.
In-fighting	Fencing at closed distance, where the distance between the two fencers is such

that the weapon must be withdrawn before the point can threaten or hit the target.

Invitation

A movement opening or leaving open a line to encourage the opponent to attack.

J

Junior

The Under 20 age-group category. Junior World Cups and World and Zonal Championships are held every year.

L

Lamé

The electrically conductive jacket worn by foil and sabre fencers. The lamé is connected to the body wire with a clip, causing it to be conductive.

Line

The main direction of an attack (for example, high/low, inside/outside), often matched to the parry that must be made to deflect the attack. Confusingly, 'line' is also used as an abbreviated version of **point-in-line** (see below).

Lines

The means of referring to a position or area on a fencer's body.

Lunge

The most basic and common attacking movement in modern fencing.

M

Maraging steel

A steel alloy used for making blades rated for international competition. Usually stronger and more durable than conventional carbon-steel blades.

Match

The aggregate of bouts or relays between two fencing teams. In the UK, 'match' is also equivalent to a 'bout' between two individuals.

N

Neuvieme   The ninth parry. A high parry used principally in foil, and equivalent to an elevated **sixte** often used to defend against a **flick**.

O

Octave   The eighth parry. A low parry used in foil and épée, covering the outside low line with the point lower than the hand.

On guard   See **En garde**

One-two   A compound attacking action consisting of a disengage-feint followed by a second disengage to deceive the opponent's parry.

Opposition   A method of executing an offensive or counter-offensive action whereby the fencer maintains blade contact throughout the action in order to control the opponent's weapon and prevent it from hitting.

Opposition parry   Deflecting the attacking blade without losing contact with the blade from the initial engagement.

P

Parry   A simple defensive action designed to deflect an attack, performed with the forte (strongest part) of the blade. There are nine basic parries, and some variations. Different schools of fencing teach slightly different positions for these parries.

Passé An attack that passes the target without hitting.

Passe avant *or* Pass forward

(Also called a 'cross-over' or 'cross step') A footwork action where the rear foot moves in front of the forward foot on the body's inside. From the crossed position, the front foot then moves forward into the 'en garde' stance. Note: Passing forward is illegal in sabre.

Patinando A step forward and lunge which can be delivered with a fast step and a lunge, or with a slow step to provoke a slower response from one's opponent or to observe their reaction, and then a fast lunge.

Pistol grip A modern grip used in foil and épée, often resembling the grip of a small pistol (generally with more protruding gripping aids than a real pistol's grip). Varieties are known by names such as Belgian, German, Russian, and Visconti.

Plastron An item of protective clothing worn under the jacket. A plastron usually consists of a sleeve and a chest/abdomen covering, which provides additional protection. A plastron should be seamless under the weapon arm, providing no stress points for a broken blade to penetrate.

Point The tip of the blade. In foil and épée, the point is the only part of the blade which can score a valid touch. The point *or* the edge of the blade may also be used in sabre.

Point-in-line

A point-in-line is created by a fencer extending their weapon with a straight arm prior to the start of any attack from their opponent. In foil and sabre, a point-in-line has right-of-way. Point-in-line is invalidated by bending the straight arm, aiming the point away from the target or withdrawing the arm, or if the opponent beats or deflects the blade.

Pommel

The fastener which is screwed onto the end of the tang, locking the guard, grip and electric connector in place. The pommel also acts as a counterweight on French grips of foils and épées, and on all sabres.

Pommelling

A method of holding a French grip further down the handle towards the pommel in order to extend the reach by a few inches

Preparation

Any action that precedes the launch of an intended attack. A preparation can be made with the blade or the feet or both.

Prêt

(French term for 'ready') Used by the referee after the command 'en garde' and before the command 'allez' ('prête' is used for women fencers).

Prime

The first parry, covering the inside low line with the guard held high and the point much lower than the hand.

Priority

In sabre and foil, equivalent to **right-of-way**. The rules that decide which fencer will be awarded a point in the event that they both touch. 'Priority' also refers to rules dealing with a tied score when time expires in foil or épée. Priority is determined randomly at the start of the last minute, and the fencer with priority wins if the score remains tied when the final minute expires.

Prise de fer (Also 'taking the blade') An engagement of the blade that attempts to control the opponent's weapon.

Pronation The position of the hand with the palm facing down.

Q

Quarte The fourth parry, covering the inside high line with the point higher than the hand.

Quinte The fifth parry. This parry, more than any other, is subject to different interpretations in the different disciplines and schools. Most commonly used in sabre to protect the head.

R

Recovery A return to the en garde stance from any other position, generally by moving back or forward into en garde after lunging.

Red card Used to punish a repeated minor rule infraction or a single major rule infraction by one of the fencers. A red card results in a point being given to the other fencer.

Referee (Also 'director' (USA) or 'president') The umpire of a fencing bout.

Renewal An offensive action made immediately after a previous attack has missed or been parried. There are three types of renewal: the remise (direct); the redoublement (indirect or compound); and the reprise (made after returning to the en garde position).

Right-of-way	See **Priority**

S

Salle	(French for 'room') A fencing hall or the venue of a fencing club.
Salute	A blade action performed before a bout or lesson to indicate respect and good sportsmanship. A handshake is also exchanged after a bout.
Second-intention	A term used to describe a fencing phrase in which the first action initiated is *not* the one intended to score. The fencer may initiate a move, anticipating, or intending to draw, a particular response from the opponent, against which a second action is planned.
Seconde	The second parry, covering the outside low line with the point lower than the hand. Used in sabre instead of octave.
Semi-circular parry	A parry that moves the blade in a semi-circle from a high line to a low line, or vice versa.
Senior	The open category. Senior World Cups and Grand Prix are held every year. Senior fencing is part of the Olympic Games, and there is a Senior World Championship in non-Olympic years.
Septime	The seventh parry, covering the inside low line, with the point lower than the hand. Used primarily in foil and épée.
Simple	An attack or riposte that involves no

feints.

Simultaneous In foil and sabre, an attack made by both fencers together for which neither fencer has earned right-of-way.

Sixte The sixth parry covering the outside high line, with the point forward and slightly above the hand; this is generally the parry taught as the basic en garde position in foil and épée.

Stop hit (Also 'stop thrust' or 'time thrust') A counter-attack into an oncoming attack; after the stop hit has landed, the fencer parries or avoids the oncoming attack.

Strip (USA) *or* **Piste** The field-of-play in which fencing takes place, measuring 14 metres long and between 1.5 and 2 metres wide. Retreating off the end of the piste with both feet results in the opponent being awarded a point. Going off the side of the piste with one or both feet halts the bout and the offending fencer is moved 1 metre back.

Supination The position of the hand when the palm is facing up.

T

Target area The valid area for scoring hits. The foil target area consists of the torso, including the groin, the part of the mask bib which covers the top of the chest, and the back. Head, arms and legs are off-target in foil. The épée target is the entire body. The sabre target is the body from hips up, except the hands and the back of the head.

Thrust   A simple attack made by moving the sword forward, with the point leading and the blade roughly parallel to the ground.

Tierce   The third parry, covering the outside high line, with the point of the weapon pointing upwards. This is also the basic en garde position in sabre.

Touche   (French for 'touch', pronounced TOOSH) Used by the referee to declare that a touch has been made. The phrase 'pas de touche' ('no touch') is used to indicate that no valid hit has been scored.

Touché   (French for 'touched', pronounced TOOSHAY) A fencer can say either 'touche' or 'touché' to acknowledge that a hit has been scored against them.

W

Whip-over   In sabre, a touch that results from the foible of the blade bending and whipping over the opponent's guard or blade when parried. Stiffer blades introduced in 1999–2000 reduced the amount of whip-overs.

Y

Yellow card   (Also **avertissement** or 'warning') A warning card issued for a minor rule infraction by one of the fencers. A second yellow card offence is punished by a red card, and thus the awarding of a point to the opponent.

From Last to First would never have come into being without the invaluable input of the following:

Jon Rhodes for his expertise and advice on the sports psychology areas of the book

Steve Petrie for his S&C and nutrition expertise and advice

Truro School for use of excellent images

Truro Fencing Club's coaches, fencers and parents

All the fencers who gave permission for their image to be used

Augusto Bizzi for image in chapter 11

Jon would like to thank Niamh for her patience and support in this and other impractical projects, Daniela for her flexible deadlines, Peter Frohlich for his insight, and the late great Richard Bonehill for unwavering belief.

Daniela would like to thank her family for inspiration, Jon for his determination and contribution to the making of great fencers, and the many fencing coaches, fencers and parents who walk this formidable path together.

10% of authors' royalties from the sale of From Last to First will be donated to the TFC Gold Foundation, a charity established in 2006 by Jon Salfield and Richard Bonehill. TFC Gold supports community-fencing projects in Cornwall, and young fencers with world-class potential.

About the authors

Jon Salfield

Jon has been a professional fencing coach for over 20 years. A former international fencer and professional musician, he is currently considered the most prolific British sabre coach of the modern era, producing a host of international fencers, who have won numerous medals on the Cadet and Junior World Cup Circuits, and reached Junior and Cadet World and European finals.

He was Team GB sabre coach at the London 2012 Olympic Games, and coached a member of Team Brazil at Rio 2016. Jon has an extraordinary breadth of experience, from teaching 6-year-olds with plastic equipment, to coaching national teams at Senior, Junior and Cadet World Championships.

From the age of 10, Jon grew up in rural Cornwall, UK. Having started his sporting life later than most, and in an environment without access to international sparring partners or coaches or a structured training program, Jon carved his own way in the sport as both an athlete and a coach.

Jon started out at the same club he heads today, Truro Fencing Club, and he and the club have grown alongside one another. Selected to represent Great Britain for the first time at the age of 30, Jon qualified for the European Championships in 2004, and went on to represent his country more than 30 times.

In his first career, as a professional musician in the field of Flamenco and World guitar music, Jon learned an enormous amount about performing under pressure, creativity, dedication to practice, and the importance of resilience and experience. Combining these lessons with his international fencing experience, the work ethic instilled in him by his first coach Richard Bonehill and the exacting technique of his last coach Peter Frohlich, has led to his style of systematic but creative fencing, which has brought some ground-breaking results for his pupils.

As well as being Head Coach at Truro Fencing Club, Jon leads the GB Sabre squad at World Cups and Championships and is the sabre Lead Coach for the British Fencing Development Program. He has written for *The Sword* magazine and appeared in films and on television as a stunt double for sword-fighting scenes. He was also featured in the DVD extras of the television series *The Borgias* and was the fencing instructor for the DVD *Learn Fencing – Advanced Sabre*.

Daniela I. Norris

Daniela is a former career diplomat, turned writer, public speaker and presenter. She is the mother of three boys – all of whom fence. Her youngest started fencing at the age of 3, and her oldest, a teenager, is a competitive fencer starting out on the international circuit. She has lived and worked in Toronto, Tel

Aviv, Jerusalem, Nairobi, Luanda, Lima, Paris and the Geneva area – and speaks six languages.

A former lieutenant in the Israeli Army, flight attendant, film translator, and diplomat with the Israeli Foreign Service, she has had dozens of works of fiction and non-fiction published in print and online, and won several literary awards for her writing.

Daniela enjoys working on both fiction and non-fiction – *From Last to First* is her third non-fiction book, and second collaborative project. She also had a collection of short stories and two novels published by John Hunt, UK.

She is an experienced public speaker with dozens of appearances before large audiences, as a diplomat and later as a writer, and also on television and radio.

A beginner fencer herself, Daniela found an interest in the sport when accompanying her fencing boys to competitions – and realising that fencing is a sport that can be commenced and practised at any age. She started fencing in her mid-forties and is hoping to soon be able to compete in the Veterans category.

Daniela also realised there was not enough guidance for parents, who end up spending thousands on equipment, coaching and competitions – without understanding the ins and outs of the sport and the kind of support their children really need.

She crossed paths and swords with Jon Salfield at Truro Fencing Club in Cornwall – and this book is the result of their collaboration.

TRANSFORMATION

Recent bestsellers from Changemakers Books are:

Integration
The Power of Being Co-Active in Work and Life
Ann Betz, Karen Kimsey-House
Integration examines how we came to be polarized in our dealing with self and other, and what we can do to move from an either/or state to a more effective and fulfilling way of being.
Paperback: 978-1-78279-865-1 ebook: 978-1-78279-866-8

Bleating Hearts
The Hidden World of Animal Suffering
Mark Hawthorne
An investigation of how animals are exploited for entertainment, apparel, research, military weapons, sport, art, religion, food, and more.
Paperback: 978-1-78099-851-0 ebook: 978-1-78099-850-3

Lead Yourself First!
Indispensable Lessons in Business and in Life
Michelle Ray
Are you ready to become the leader of your own life? Apply simple, powerful strategies to take charge of yourself, your career, your destiny.
Paperback: 978-1-78279-703-6 ebook: 978-1-78279-702-9

Burnout to Brilliance
Strategies for Sustainable Success
Jayne Morris
Routinely running on reserves? This book helps you transform your life from burnout to brilliance with strategies for sustainable success.
Paperback: 978-1-78279-439-4 ebook: 978-1-78279-438-7

Goddess Calling
Inspirational Messages & Meditations of Sacred Feminine
Liberation Thealogy
Rev. Dr. Karen Tate
A book of messages and meditations using Goddess archetypes
and mythologies, aimed at educating and inspiring those with
the desire to incorporate a feminine face of God into their
spirituality.
Paperback: 978-1-78279-442-4 ebook: 978-1-78279-441-7

The Master Communicator's Handbook
Teresa Erickson, Tim Ward
Discover how to have the most communicative impact in this
guide by professional communicators with over 30 years of
experience advising leaders of global organizations.
Paperback: 978-1-78535-153-2 ebook: 978-1-78535-154-9

Meditation in the Wild
Buddhism's Origin in the Heart of Nature
Charles S. Fisher Ph.D.
A history of Raw Nature as the Buddha's first teacher, inspiring
some followers to retreat there in search of truth.
Paperback: 978-1-78099-692-9 ebook: 978-1-78099-691-2

Ripening Time
Inside Stories for Aging with Grace
Sherry Ruth Anderson
Ripening Time gives us an indispensable guidebook for growing
into the deep places of wisdom as we age.
Paperback: 978-1-78099-963-0 ebook: 978-1-78099-962-3

Striking at the Roots
A Practical Guide to Animal Activism
Mark Hawthorne
A manual for successful animal activism from an author with
first-hand experience speaking out on behalf of animals.
Paperback: 978-1-84694-091-0 ebook: 978-1-84694-653-0

Readers of ebooks can buy or view any of these bestsellers by
clicking on the live link in the title. Most titles are published
in paperback and as an ebook. Paperbacks are available in
traditional bookshops. Both print and ebook formats are available
online.

Find more titles and sign up to our readers' newsletter at
http://www.johnhuntpublishing.com/transformation
Follow us on Facebook at
https://www.facebook.com/Changemakersbooks